Understanding Autism
A Neurodiversity Affirming Guidebook for Children and Teens

Robert Jason Grant

AutPlay® Publishing

Understanding Autism:
A Neurodiversity Affirming Guidebook for Children and Teens

©2021, 2018 Robert Jason Grant EdD
Springfield, Missouri: AutPlay® Publishing
A Robert Jason Grant EdD Product

All rights reserved. No part of this book may be reproduced, stored in a retrieval system, or transmitted, in any form or by any means, electronic, mechanical, photo copying, microfilming, recording, or otherwise, without written permission of the author.

Inventories, worksheets, and handouts may be reproduced only within the confines of the use with clients. This limited permission does not grant other rights, nor does it give permission for commercial, resale, syndication, or any other use not contained above. Any other use, or reproduction, is a violation of international laws and is forbidden without express written permission from the author.

ISBN: 9781732909922

All Images Provided by ClipArtLord.com, free images, or Robert Jason Grant Ed.D

Correspondence regarding this book:
Robert Jason Grant EdD/AutPlay® Publishing
info@autplaytherapy.com
www.robertjasongrant.com
www.autplaytherapy.com

For Joey

What Others Are Saying

Having a tool to start a discussion about autism is a great thing to build understanding and improve personal confidence. This book is such a tool for this type of discussion. Parents and professionals are encouraged to use the guidebook as an interactive tool to discuss some of the uniqueness of the characteristics of autism spectrum disorder. Grab the color pencils, paints, colors, and markers as well as this guidebook and let the discussion begin.
–Shelli Allen
Creator of Steps Care Inc. and Author, *Steps: Forming a Disability Ministry*

This guidebook is fantastic! I especially love how children and teens can use this book to explore their interests and feelings related to their perception of what it means to be autistic. Partnering with parents in this way to provide a resource that educates the whole family about autism yet keeps the focus on highlighting the distinct interests and strengths of the child is brilliant!
–Amy Vaughan, OTR/L, BCP
Author, *Positively Sensory*

There are few resources specific to Autism that are as comprehensive, and yet as facilitative as this new resource. Dr. Robert Jason Grant has developed an area of expertise in the combination of play therapy and autism. This guidebook is helpful for guiding children and teens who want to come to an understanding about their own diagnosis. The in-depth explanation of autism is helpful for the practitioner and caregiver, while the worksheets are helpful for therapeutic psychoeducation for the child. Each section is like taking a self-guided tour through the mystery of autism.
–Patricia Gilbaugh, Ph.D., LISW, RPT-S, CAS
Executive Director, Grace C Mae Advocate Center, Inc.

Dr. Robert Grant, in his guidebook, addresses important issues concerning autistic children and teens. In this succinct, yet thorough book, Grant clearly describes autism basics, for both parents and professionals. The book provides guided opportunities for children to work through and discuss the various aspects of autism, in a way that is both encouraging and informative. We have all been waiting for a non-threatening method of talking about the issues of autism. Grant takes the mystery out of autism, gives space for personal reflection and opinion, and brings the child to a point of accepting their wonderful self, and the differences that exist on the spectrum. This should be required curricula for all parents and teens.
–Dayna Ault
Creator/Owner, The Missouri Autism Report

UNDERSTANDING AUTISM

Our knowledge and understanding of autism has evolved over the years as more and more autistic adults are publicly sharing their experiences and opinions about therapy approaches that were previously held in high regard as the "gold standard." Recognizing the need for a shift in how autism is understood and conceptualized, Dr. Grant has created an excellent tool to help us better understand the complexity of autism with well laid out information written in such clear, easy to understand terms. He does a great job highlighting the need to ensure affirming approaches help children and teens appreciate their neurodiversity and value themselves from a strengths based approach.
-Annette Brandenburg
Creator/President, Southwest Autism Network of Missouri (SWAN)

As an autistic individual with an autistic son, I wish this had been the first book that I read on our journey. I feel the first days of an autism diagnosis is the most scary, because we want to know, "What's next?" This book is so helpful, and it reminded me again how proud I am to be autistic, and quirky, and to be myself. I especially appreciate the section on finding affirming therapies. I think as parents we need to know the right questions to ask, and that we can easily get misguided by the title of a therapy program, and to remember to always be led from the child/client. Reading from autistic voices truly made me feel seen and heard in this book and I could very much relate to what was spoken here, and I truly feel reading this guidebook made me cry happy tears that I was enough, and my son read the excerpt from Kyle and said "I'm proud to be autistic mom, and that there are others like me." I especially loved that this book took a stance on tokenism, and just because you know one autistic child does not mean you know them all, and to value the lived in experience from an autistic individual above all else.
- Kellie Harding, MSW LICSW-A

A breath of fresh air! Dr. Grant's revised guidebook, Understanding Autism: A Neurodiversity Affirming Guidebook for Children and Teens, embodies Maya Angelou's wisdom, "Do the best you can until you know better. Then when you know better, do better." Dr. Grant's use of neurodiversity affirming language, focus on strengths, and incorporation of autistic voices is both refreshing and necessary as we work towards a more informed perspective for supporting autistics in the area of mental health.
-Katie Bassiri, LPCC, RPT-S, ACAS
Owner and Executive Director, The Treehouse

Contents

Autism 1
    A Medical Model Perspective 1
    Evaluation and Diagnosis: An Alternative Presentation 4
    A Non-Pathology Affirming Perspective 7
    Important Terminology 11
Therapies Involving Autistic Children and Teens 14
    Affirming Therapies 15
    Possible Needs 16
A Focus on Strengths 20
Living Autistic in a Non-Autistic World 22
    Listening to Autistic Voices: Anastasia Phelps 24
    Listening To Autistic Voices: Kyle Calderon 26
Valuing the Autistic Child 30
How to Use This Guidebook 32
The Worksheets 33
This Guidebook Is Designed to Help You Understand Yourself and Autism 34
What Does Autism Mean? 37
What Are Some of Your Questions About Autism? 41
What Are Your Feelings About Being Autistic? 43
What Are Some Things That Might Be Part of Being Autistic? 47
How Do You Think You Became Autistic? Will You Always Be Autistic? 50
Do You Know an Autistic Person? 53
What Does Spectrum Mean in Autism Spectrum Disorder? 56
Where You Are on the Spectrum Sometimes Depends on the Strengths and Needs You have. What Strengths Do You Think You Have? 58
What Needs Do You Think You Have? 61
Is There Something You Believe You Are Not Good at That You Want to Improve? 63
Do You Think Being Autistic Is Good, Bad, or You're Not Sure? 66

UNDERSTANDING AUTISM

Does Being Autistic Make You Different From Other Children? 68
Are There Certain Things You Can Do (Strengths) Because You Are Autistic? 70
What Is It Like Playing With Other Kids When You Are Autistic? 72
What Do You Like to Do for Fun? 77
What Animal Do You Think You Are Most Like and Why? 80
If You Could Jump into Any Video Game, What One Would It Be and Why? 82
Does the Place You Are in (Home, School, Church) Make a Difference If You Are Autistic? 84
Who Helps Autistic Children? 86
Does Being Autistic Mean There Are Things You Can't Do or Things You Might Do Better Than Other People? 88
Do You Know Any Famous Autistic People? If So, List Them Below. 91
What Do You Want Others to Know About You? 93
What Do You Wish Others Understood About Autism? 95
Let's Write a Letter Describing You to Someone. 97
What Are Some Things You Want to Remember That Make You Feel Good? 99
Some Things About Being Autistic Can Be Awesome! 101
Appendix: Resources 103
Learning About Autism Social Story 104
My Autistic Snapshot 105
AutPlay® Autism Checklist–Revised 107
   About the AutPlay® Autism Checklist-R 108
Identity Language Article 109
Feeling List 112
AWESOME Autism Books for Children 113
AWESOME Autism Books for Teens 114
AWESOME Websites for Children and Teens 115
AWESOME YouTube Channels 115
AWESOME Autism Apps for Children and Teens 116
AWESOME Autism Games for Children 117
AWESOME Neurodiversity Affirming Resources 118

References	119
About Dr. Robert Jason Grant	122
Additional Products by Dr. Robert Jason Grant	123
The Virtual Sandtray App AutPlay Package	124
The AutPlay® Therapy Certification Program	125
Notes Sheets	126

It is not our differences that divide us. It is our inability to recognize, accept, and celebrate those differences.
— Audre Lorde

Understanding Autism

A Neurodiversity Affirming Guidebook for Children and Teens

Autism

When working with autistic children and teens and especially as you might use this guidebook, it is important to have an awareness and appreciation for the autistic client. The production of information about autism is quite prolific. Finding books, articles, blogs, websites, podcasts, videos, etc. talking about and attempting to explain autism is extremely easy. Although there is a wealth of resources related to describing autism, this does not mean the information is always accurate or productive in helping the actual autistic child or teen. This guidebook will attempt to add to the options with a focus on highlighting different views of autism, especially the views of actual autistics and those who work from a neurodiversity affirming framework and philosophy.

A Medical Model Perspective

The Autism Society of America (2021) describes itself as one of the oldest grassroots autism organizations that works to improve the quality of life for all affected by autism. The organization defines autism as a

> complex, lifelong developmental disability that typically appears during early childhood and can impact a person's social skills, communication, relationships, and self-regulation. Autism is defined by a certain set of behaviors and is a "spectrum condition" that affects people differently and to varying degrees (para. 1).

The Centers for Disease Control and Prevention (CDC) (2021) proposed that autism spectrum disorder is "a developmental disability that can cause significant social, communication, and behavioral challenges" (para. 1). There is often nothing about how people with autism look that sets them apart from other people, but people with autism may communicate, interact, behave, and learn in ways that are different from most other people. The learning, thinking, and problem-solving abilities of people with autism can range from gifted to severely challenged. Some people with autism need a lot of help in their daily lives; others need less.

Many organizations, groups, and agencies have historically viewed autism through a medical model influenced by the American Psychiatric Association's Diagnostic and Statistical Manual (DSM), which is the guide in the United States for providing a formal diagnosis of autism. The medical model looks at autism as a set of deficits or impairments. Under the medical model, these impairments or differences should be "fixed" or changed by medical and other treatments, even when the impairment or difference does not cause pain or illness. The medical model looks at what is "wrong" with the person, instead of strengths or what that person needs.

Professionals and parents should understand that the current system supports a diagnosis of autism typically made through a thorough psychological evaluation conducted by a trained psychologist, which would be a *medical diagnosis*. Schools may also implement testing to diagnose for autism, which would be an *educational diagnosis*. Psychiatrists, neurologists, and medical doctors can provide a medical autism diagnosis. The psychological evaluation process typically includes several assessment/evaluation inventories, can take anywhere from three hours to two days to complete, and is based on the DSM criteria and process.

Two inventories used to diagnose autism are considered gold-standard inventories. *Gold standard* means these inventories have validity and reliability measures to produce the best, most accurate assessment for diagnosis. The two inventories for autism that are considered gold standard are the Autism Diagnostic Observation Schedule (ADOS) and the Autism Diagnostic Interview–Revised (ADI-R). Other popular inventories may be used as well, such as the Childhood Autism Rating Scale (CARS). A reliable and accurate diagnosis of autism can be acquired as early as 18 months of age. However, many individuals with autism do not receive a formal autism diagnosis at 18 months of age; most diagnoses of autism occur between the ages of 4.5 and 5.5.

Typically, the process of a formal psychological evaluation diagnosis of autism uses the protocol outlined in the DSM and thus works out of a medical model, which views autism as problematic, highlighting deficits and struggles and the need to cure or correct deficits. A synopsis of the *Diagnostic and Statistical Manual* 5th Edition (2014) criteria for receiving an autism diagnosis is presented below:

A. Persistent deficits in social communication and social interaction across multiple contexts, as manifested by the following, currently or by history:
   1. Deficits in social-emotional reciprocity; for example, abnormal social approach and failure of normal back-and-forth conversation; reduced sharing of interests, emotions, or affect; and failure to initiate or respond to social interactions.
   2. Deficits in nonverbal communicative behaviors used for social interaction; for example, poorly integrated verbal and nonverbal communication; abnormalities in eye contact and body language or deficits in understanding and use of gestures; and a total lack of facial expressions and nonverbal communication.
   3. Deficits in developing, maintaining, and understanding relationships; for example, difficulties adjusting behavior to suit various social contexts; difficulties in sharing imaginative play or in making friends; and absence of interest in peers.

UNDERSTANDING AUTISM

B. Restricted, repetitive patterns of behavior, interests, or activities, as manifested by at least two of the following, currently or by history:
  1. Stereotyped or repetitive motor movements, use of objects, or speech (e.g., simple motor stereotypies, lining up toys or flipping objects, echolalia, idiosyncratic phrases).
  2. Insistence on sameness, inflexible adherence to routines, or ritualized patterns of verbal or nonverbal behavior (e.g., extreme distress at small changes, difficulties with transitions, rigid thinking patterns, greeting rituals, need to take same route or eat same food every day).
  3. Highly restricted, fixated interests that are abnormal in intensity or focus (e.g., strong attachment to or preoccupation with unusual objects, excessively circumscribed or perseverative interest).
  4. Hyper- or hyporeactivity to sensory input or unusual interests in sensory aspects of the environment (e.g., apparent indifference to pain/temperature, adverse response to specific sounds or textures, excessive smelling or touching of objects, visual fascination with lights or movement).
C. Symptoms must be present in the early developmental period (but may not become fully manifest until social demands exceed limited capacities or may be masked by learned strategies in later life).
D. Symptoms cause clinically significant impairment in social, occupational, or other important areas of current functioning.
E. These disturbances are not better explained by intellectual disability (intellectual developmental disorder) or global developmental delay. Intellectual disability and autism spectrum disorder frequently co-occur; to make comorbid diagnoses of autism spectrum disorder and intellectual disability, social communication should be below that expected for general developmental level.

There are three levels in the DSM 5. The levels describe support needs for those given a diagnosis of autism. They are defined as follows:

Level 3: Requiring Very Substantial Support
Severe deficits in verbal and nonverbal social communication skills cause severe impairments in functioning; very limited initiation of social interactions; minimal response to social overtures from others.

For example, a person with few words of intelligible speech who rarely initiates interaction and, when he or she does, makes unusual approaches to meet needs only and responds to only very direct social approaches.

Inflexibility of behavior, extreme difficulty coping with change, or other restricted/repetitive behaviors markedly interfere with functioning in all spheres. Great distress/difficulty changing focus or action.

Level 2: Requiring Substantial Support
Marked deficits in verbal and nonverbal social communication skills; social impairments apparent even with supports in place; limited initiation of social interactions; and reduced or abnormal responses to social overtures from others.

For example, a person who speaks in simple sentences, whose interaction is limited to narrow special interests, and who has markedly odd nonverbal communication.

Inflexibility of behavior, difficulty coping with change, or other restricted/repetitive behaviors appear frequently enough to be obvious to the casual observer and interfere with functioning in a variety of contexts. Distress and/or difficulty changing focus or action.

Level 1: Requiring Support
Without supports in place, deficits in social communication cause noticeable impairments; difficulty initiating social interactions and clear examples of atypical or unsuccessful responses to social overtures of others; may appear to have decreased interest in social interactions.

For example, a person who can speak in full sentences and engages in communication but whose to-and-fro conversation with others fails and whose attempts to make friends are odd and typically unsuccessful.

Inflexibility of behavior causes significant interference with functioning in one or more contexts. Difficulty switching between activities. Problems of organization and planning hamper independence.

Evaluation and Diagnosis: An Alternative Presentation

Brown et al. (2021) proposed that solely deficit-framed descriptions often miss the strengths that can be associated with autism. While autistic children may have more challenges than neurotypical children, the overall well-being of autistic children and their families is harmed when we frame autism in terms of deficits. An alternative framing could, as soon as the family begins the diagnostic process, use a strengths-based approach and draw on the idea of neurodiversity. Brown et al. (2021) further provided suggestions for diagnosticians who are sharing a diagnosis of autism with families. They state it is imperative for assessors to have training and support in how to communicate

UNDERSTANDING AUTISM

assessment results with families in a meaningful, respectful, and supportive way and provided several guidelines to consider:

Remember that words are powerful—The way the diagnostician tells *the story of autism* makes a difference. Consider the terms used to describe a child and the diagnosis of autism from a neurodiversity perspective. For example, instead of using the word *deficit*, try *needs*; instead of *co-morbid*, try *co-occurring*; and for very young children, consider using *high probability* of autism, rather than *at-risk*. These subtle changes in vocabulary communicate to families that their child is more than a label and is still the same child that came to the clinic with them prior to the diagnosis.

Partner with parents during disclosure: Ask parents how they feel about receiving a diagnosis and what they already think and know about autism. This will help identify where parents may need more information and support. Parents may also need information about autism, understanding why their child fits with this diagnosis, and what would be their next steps – ideally pursing neurodiversity affirming services.

Set a positive and warm tone: A warm and positive clinician can mitigate parents' emotional reactions after disclosure and help parents identify strengths in their children and in their own skills as parents. Get to know the child and family and provide feedback in an empathetic and respectful way to acknowledge parent concerns and feelings while also sharing strengths.

Be honest and remain hopeful: We must balance discussion of strengths with acknowledgement of a child's needs—in terms of both learning (such as intellectual disabilities) and the environment (such as a need for additional support). Parents come to the assessment because of concerns and ignoring those concerns may leave parents feeling unheard and undervalued. Challenges can be acknowledged in context of a whole child with strengths and weaknesses that can be harnessed or supported.

Consider how intervention/therapies are presented: Many families receive an autism diagnosis for their child and immediately begin a journey of seeking more and more hours of intervention to "cure" their children. While beginning intervention early is certainly important, data do not support the idea that highly intensive, highly structured intervention will promote advancement. Rather than talking about recovery, discuss intervention as a way to increase adaptive skills and promote quality of life. Early autism intervention research has become more naturalistic, valuing, and child affirming while remaining highly effective at increasing communication and supporting social interactions and play that build on a child's strengths and interests rather than "curing" them.

Consider intersectionality: Diagnostic disclosure should be done using culturally responsive and sensitive practices. Depending on their culture, families may have a history of negative interactions with health care providers and a general mistrust in the system (Moseley et al., 2007) or may feel undervalued or unheard by medical professionals—especially if their initial concerns were not taken seriously. Autism may be stigmatized in some cultures, which may necessitate taking more care in how the diagnosis is disclosed.

Address caregivers' support needs: Parents of autistic children often experience greater stress than parents of neurotypical children. Caregivers often experience a lack of support; negative judgements and affiliate stigma from friends, family, and the community at large; and added financial burden. Given all these impacts, many parents may urgently need support and validation. There needs not be any conflict between encouraging positive views of autism and recognizing the challenges that caregivers face in our society.

Grant (2021) proposed a strengths-based autism screening inventory (AutPlay® Autism Checklist Revised), which explores the possibility that a child may have autism from a strengths perspective instead of looking for deficits. The inventory considers descriptors such as *seems to have their own way of communicating and interacting*, *prefers constructive play* (Legos, blocks, train track), *has an intense focus on specific things or subjects*, and *not as interested in social processes that may be common with peers*. The Autplay® Autism Checklist Revised can be found in the appendix section of this workbook and on the Resources page of the AutPlay® Therapy website (www.autplaytherapy.com).

Lowry (2021), an autistic psychologist, developed a reframe of DSM autistic traits from a strengths-based (Strengths-Based Autism Diagnostic Criteria) rather than a deficits-based perspective. He presents the following strengths-based view of diagnosing autism:

I. To meet diagnostic criteria for autism according to DSM-5, a child must have persistent differences in each of three areas of social communication and interaction (see A1–A3 below) plus at least two of four types of repetitive behaviors (see B1–B4 below).

   A. Different social communication and interaction as evidenced by the following:

1. Differences in communication—tendency to go off on tangents, tendency to talk passionately about special interests, and tendency to not engage in small talk.
2. Differences in nonverbal communication, including stimming while talking, looking at something else while talking, and being bored with conversations.
3. Due to the above differences in communication, autistic people tend to be shunned by neurotypicals and, therefore, are conditioned to believe that they are somehow less social.

B. Repetitive behavior or interests as evidenced by at least two of the following:

1. Stimming or engaging in echolalia.
2. Security in routines. Autistic people do not have a sensory filter, so the world is perceived as a constant state of chaos. Routines and expectations give comfort to overwhelmed autistic people.
3. Special Interests (SPINS). Due to hyperconnected brains, autistic people feel more passionately about what they love, so when they have a special interest, they tend to fawn over and fixate on it.
4. Hyper- or hyporeactivity to stimuli. Again, due to hyperconnections, they feel emotions more intensely. Sometimes, they feel emotions less intensely because they tune them out in favor of other stimuli.

II. Autistic people are born with these traits but learn how to mask them. Sometimes, the traits show up only when they are stressed and let down their guards.

III. These traits cause other people distress. Note the DSM ONLY indicates impairment when it affects other people or jobs, but not when it is a daily issue that the autistic person learns to live with.

IV. Autism is not due to intellectual disability.

A Non-Pathology Affirming Perspective

The Autism Self Advocacy Network (ASAN) (2021) is an organization run by and for autistic people. ASAN was created to serve as a national grassroots disability rights organization for the autistic community. The organization seeks to advance the principles of the disability rights movement regarding autism. ASAN defines autism as the following:

Autism is a developmental disability that affects how we experience the world around us. Autistic people are an important part of the world. Autism is a normal part of life and makes us who we are.

Autism has always existed. Autistic people are born autistic, and we will be autistic our whole lives. Autism can be diagnosed by a doctor, but you can be autistic even if you don't have a formal diagnosis. Because of myths about autism, it can be harder for autistic adults, autistic girls, and autistic people of color to get a diagnosis. But anyone can be autistic, regardless of race, gender, or age.

Autistic people are in every community, and we always have been. Autistic people are people of color. Autistic people are immigrants. Autistic people are a part of every religion, every income level, and every age group. Autistic people are women. Autistic people are queer, and autistic people are trans. Autistic people are often many of these things at once. The communities we are a part of and the ways we are treated shape what autism is like for us.

There is no one way to be autistic. Some autistic people can speak, and some autistic people need to communicate in other ways. Some autistic people also have intellectual disabilities, and some autistic people don't. Some people need a lot of help in their day-to-day lives, and some autistic people only need a little help. All of these people are autistic, because there is no right or wrong way to be autistic. All of us experience autism differently, but we all contribute to the world in meaningful ways. (paras. 1–4)

ASAN (2021) further explains that autistic people deserve understanding and acceptance. Every autistic person experiences autism differently, but there are some things that many have in common. Autistic individuals—

- think differently
- process senses differently
- move differently
- communicate differently
- socialize differently
- might need help with daily living

The Autistic Women and Nonbinary Network (AWN) 2021, an organization dedicated to building a supportive community that provides support and resources for autistic women, girls, transfeminine and transmasculine nonbinary people, and trans people of all genders, stated:

Autism is a pervasive developmental disability that impacts communication, movement, and sensory processing. "Pervasive" means that autism affects every

> part of us because it is our neurology. Autistic people are as diverse as any other group of people and we each have our own strengths and weaknesses.
>
> The amount of support that each autistic person needs can vary greatly between individuals and even in the same person from day to day. However, each one of us experiences and interprets the world around us in distinctly autistic ways. (p. 8)

Walker (2021) defined autism as follows: Autism is a genetically based human neurological variant. The complex set of interrelated characteristics that distinguish autistic neurology from non-autistic neurology is not yet fully understood, but current evidence indicates that the central distinction is that autistic brains are characterized by particularly high levels of synaptic connectivity and responsiveness. This tends to make the autistic individual's subjective experience more intense and chaotic than that of non-autistic individuals: on both the sensorimotor and cognitive levels, the autistic mind tends to register more information, and the impact of each bit of information tends to be both stronger and less predictable. Autism is a developmental phenomenon, meaning that it begins in utero and has a pervasive influence on development, on multiple levels, throughout the lifespan. Autism produces distinctive, atypical ways of thinking, moving, interacting, and sensory and cognitive processing. One analogy that has often been made is that autistic individuals have a different neurological *operating system* than non-autistic individuals. Despite underlying neurological commonalities, autistic individuals are vastly different from one another. Some autistic individuals exhibit exceptional cognitive talents. However, in the context of a society designed around the sensory, cognitive, developmental, and social needs of non-autistic individuals, autistic individuals are almost always disabled to some degree—sometimes quite obviously, and sometimes more subtly.

Cruz (2021) explained that the diagnostic criteria and symptomology of autism is based on young white males. Due to being based on a specific race and gender, it isn't easily put into context of other cultures; we do not often see how it looks for non-white, non-male children. As much of the focus of what autism is and looks like centers on the DSM and a medical model, it is easy to see how much gets lost in understanding autistic children and how frustrated autistic individuals must feel in not being fully seen and understood. As we strive to work out of a neurodiversity-affirming philosophy, we must look holistically at the autistic child—who they are, what their preferences and interests are, what they do well, what their strengths are, and how historically perceived deficits are possibly strengths or, at the very least, differences in being and not problematic. We must commit to understanding the child's needs that may warrant therapy but within a context of person/situation needs—not autistic needs.

The Art of Autism (2021) stated that autism needs to be considered through the social model of disability, which "underpins the concept of neurodiversity:"

> The social model looks at how we can accommodate autistic people in society. It identifies systemic barriers, negative attitudes, and exclusion by society (purposely or inadvertently). While physical, sensory, intellectual, or psychological variations may cause individual functional limitation or impairments, these do not have to lead to disability unless society fails to take account of, include, and accommodate people regardless of their individual differences. (para. 5)

The social model of disability says that disability is caused by the way society is organized. It identifies systemic barriers, negative attitudes, and exclusion by society (purposely or inadvertently) that mean society is the main contributory factor in disabling people. A social model perspective does not deny the reality of impairment nor its impact on the individual. However, it does challenge the physical, attitudinal, communication, and social environment to accommodate impairment as an expected incident of human diversity. The social model seeks to change society in order to accommodate people living with impairment; it does not seek to change persons with impairment to accommodate society (People with Disability Australia, 2021).

Goering (2015) stated that the social model of disability focuses attention on the attitudinal obstacles faced by people with non-standard bodies. Other people's expectations about quality of life, ability to work, etc. for a person with a disability not only affect the ways in which physical structures and institutional norms are made and sustained (based on presumptions about inability to perform), but also can create additional disability by making it harder for such individuals to feel good about themselves. The social model reminds us to be careful about what we presume to be irremediable through social change and to question the ways in which we currently understand disability. Challenging standard definitions of disability and impairment will require listening carefully to the experiences of people living with those impairments and thinking creatively about possibilities for inclusion, accommodation, and accessibility.

Consider this simple but clear example of the social model of disability: the case of Adam, an autistic teen who was attending a public high school. As a freshman in high school, Adam was testing at a 3rd grade level in math (which he had been testing at since 3rd grade). Adam's mother sought tutoring services outside of the school to help Adam increase his math skills. Upon participation with special tutors, it was discovered that if Adam could use a calculator to complete his math work, he scored at a 9th grade level in math—five grade levels higher than he was scoring in public school testing processes. It was further discovered that some of Adam's school teachers had recognized that Adam could do more advanced math when he used a calculator vs. pencil-and-paper equation operations, but they felt he needed to learn how to do math the way they were teaching it and did not and would not allow him to use a calculator. In summary, Adam did not have a math disability. He could comprehend and perform math equations at grade level when allowed to use a calculator. It was his environment (societal perspective that using a calculator was invalid) that was disabling him from advancing in math ability.

Important Terminology

Neurodiversity: In the 1990s, an autistic sociologist named Judy Singer coined the term *neurodiversity*. Neurodiversity is an approach to learning and disability that argues diverse neurological conditions are a result of normal variations in the human genome. Every person is part of neurodiversity; we all have a unique way that our brain is wired to operate and navigate. Nelson (2020) expressed that neurodiversity is respect, and respect is everything that comes with a world built for the diverse people who inhabit it. It is widespread access to many forms of communication. It is systems built and modified with the involvement of the diverse people those systems will serve.

Neurodiversity affirming: A belief and commitment in approach, which means valuing and respecting the different ways an autistic or neurodivergent client may process, feel, respond, communicate, and play. It means allowing the child to be themselves and not trying to change them to fit a neurotypical standard. Further, it means giving the client a voice in the decision-making process regarding their therapy.

Ableism: The discrimination against people with disabilities—harboring beliefs that devalue and limit the potential of people with physical, intellectual, or mental disorders and disabilities (Vormer, 2020). The belief (consciously aware or conditioned) that those without disability are superior. Ableism practices can sometimes be conditioned, with individuals participating in ableist behaviors without realizing.

Vormer (2020) provided some questions to ask in checking your own ableist biases. It may be necessary to do some work eradicating your own ableist views if you find yourself answering yes to any of the following:
- Do you feel that people with disabilities need to be cured?
- Do you think that all disabled people have intellectual challenges?
- Do you think that people with disabilities can't be full members of society?
- Do you feel pity for people with disabilities?
- Do you think that all people with disabilities rely on other people their whole life?
- Do you believe that a person's disability is the most important thing about them?

Neurotypical: A term used to describe individuals who are not neurodivergent and of societal-viewed typical development, intellect, and cognitive abilities.

Neurodivergent: Refers to a mind that functions in ways that diverge significantly from the dominant societal standards of what is normal and expected. This often includes diagnoses such as autism, ADHD, and learning disorders.

Neurodiversity paradigm: A perspective on neurodiversity that includes the belief that all humans are diverse in their neurocognitive functioning; there is no one normal standard for neurocognitive functioning.

Neurodiversity movement: A social justice movement that seeks civil rights, equality, respect, and full societal inclusion for the neurodivergent.

Non-autistic: Anyone who does not have autism. This can include neurodivergent individuals who are not autistic but have some other neurodivergence.

Medical model of disability: Regarding autism, this model views autism as a disorder, something that is a problem that needs to be fixed, treated, or cured.

Social model of disability: Regarding autism, this model views autism as a person's identity and not what makes a person disabled. Rather, it is society's views of autism that makes an autistic person disabled.

Strengths-based approach: Taking an approach that involves looking at a child's strengths and building upon their strengths to help address their needs. Rapp, Saleebey, and Sullivan (2008) suggested six standards for determining a strengths-based approach. If in agreement, practitioners can use the following list when considering the method they will use when practicing the strengths-based approach:

1. **Goal orientation:** It is crucial and vital for the person to set goals.
2. **Strengths assessment:** The person finds and assesses their strengths and inherent resources.
3. **Resources from the environment:** Connect resources in the person's environment that can be useful or enable the person to create links to these resources. The resources could be individuals, associations, institutions, or groups.
4. **Different methods are used first for different situations:** Clients will determine goals first and then strengths that can be used. In strengths-based case management, individuals determine their strengths by first using an assessment.

UNDERSTANDING AUTISM

5. **The relationship is hope-inducing**: By finding strengths and linking to connections (with other people, communities, or culture), the client finds hope.
6. **Meaningful choice:** Each person is an expert on their strengths, resources, and hopes. It is the practitioner's duty to improve upon choices the person makes and encourage making informed decisions.

Masking: The act of hiding autism features and/or characteristics. Also, hiding one's identity as being autistic. This is typically done in response to neurotypical expectations to act a certain way. Over time, this process can become psychologically distressing to autistic individuals.

Actually autistic: A term that refers to individuals who are autistic and who speak from their perspective of being autistic.

Identity-first language: Using language that places a person's identity first such as saying, "autistic child" or "autistic person." Research supports that the majority of autistic adults prefer identity first language over person-first language (child with autism). This workbook defaults to identity-first language as it is the preference for the population being discussed. For more information about identity-first language, read the resource in the appendix section titled *Play Therapists and the Terminology of Autism*.

Therapies Involving Autistic Children and Teens

There exist a significant number of purported autism "treatments." Many of the most recognized and/or evidence-based purported "treatments" consist of behavioral methods, social skills training, and developmental approaches. Bio-medical and existential approaches also exist. Actual autistics and neurodiversity affirming advocates resist the notion of "treatment" for autism. There is no cure for autism, and autism is not a disease. The terms *therapy* or *support* are much preferred and more affirming than the term treatment. Further, the proposition that an autistic child automatically needs a certain therapy because they are autistic is an ableist concept and can be detrimental to the child's wellbeing. An autistic child or teen does not enter a therapy because they are autistic. They enter a therapy because they have a need that the therapy can help address.

Siri and Lyons (2010) suggested that since the etiology as well as the manifestations of autism are influenced by a variety of multiple factors, a one-size-fits-all approach to interventions is not the most beneficial approach. No two children will have the same therapy needs or respond to the same combination of therapies. Each child's therapy plan needs to be unique, taking into consideration the child's specific strengths, needs, culture, and family dynamics. Many autistic children will participate in some type of program, therapy, or intervention. The variety and depth of the service can look different for each child.

It would be easy to produce a list of over 100 promoted and advertised therapies, or services focused on autistic children. The variety of options include biomedical, behavioral, developmental, alternative, and difficult-to-categorize interventions. With the plethora of autism-focused services bombarding parents and considering the vulnerability issues many parents struggle with in wanting to provide beneficial supports for their child, it becomes essential to critically evaluate promoted services geared toward autistic children and their families. The following guide can serve as a beginning protocol for evaluating services.

1. What does the research say about the promoted service? Is there any research support? Does the service incorporate any evidence for addressing what it promotes? Remember that a therapy approach may be helpful even if it is not evidence based, but it is important to know what research has been presented on the approach. Also, remember that historically (and often still in present day), research specifically focused on autistic children has been ladened with ableist

bias. For research specific to the autistic population, it would be important to consider neurodiversity affirming research.
2. What are the potential risks of participating in the therapy? Are there any potentially dangerous side effects? Can any harm be done to the child or family? If a therapy approach contains possible harm or risk to the child, it should be highly scrutinized before beginning.
3. What is the cost of the therapy? How much money will the family have to pay out of pocket to receive the therapy? It is important to be aware that some therapies may exist to take advantage of families. The cost of the therapy should be within reason for the type of service that is being provided.
4. Does the therapy promise to cure autism or take the autism away? What are the proposed benefits of participating in the therapy? What are the therapy outcomes? Does the therapy make any promises? If so, what are the promises? Any therapy that promises to cure autism or promises absolutes in gains should be avoided. Therapy should also have an evaluation component that can be explained to families.
5. Does the therapy seem like a good fit for the child and the family considering financial demands, time demands, and therapy expectations/processes? Families should consider if the therapy approach is something the family can commit their time, finances, and energy to before beginning.
6. How is the therapy governed or monitored? Families should understand if there is any oversite for the therapy or the professional providing the therapy. Families should also understand if they can observe or be a part of the therapy in which their child is participating. If the therapy has no accountability or parents are not allowed to observe or participate, this may be a caution for families regarding the therapy.
7. How is the professional implementing the therapy considered a valid and reliable person to do so? Professionals or those implementing therapy should be able to communicate to families how they are qualified to implement the therapy.
8. What do actual autistics say about certain therapies, especially therapies they have participated in as children? Why is the therapy beneficial for the child? What are the child's actual needs that align with the therapy?

Affirming Therapies

Some common affirming therapies are listed below with a brief description. Professionals and parents should be cautioned that each individual therapist or professional needs to be reviewed for affirming practices. Some simple questions to ask the professional could be—
- What is your view on neurodiversity?
- Do you implement neurodiversity affirming practices?
- How are you neurodiversity affirming?
- Can you give me some examples?

Play Therapy: The Association for Play Therapy (2021) defines play therapy as the systematic use of a theoretical model to establish an interpersonal process wherein trained play therapists use the therapeutic powers of play to help clients prevent or resolve psychosocial difficulties and achieve optimal growth and development. There exist several affirming play therapy theories and approaches such as AutPlay® Therapy, which is designed to address mental health needs of autistic and neurodivergent children. Certified AutPlay® Therapy professionals implement a variety of play therapy approaches and interventions to address needs such as regulation struggles, anxiety issues, trauma, and self-advocacy (Grant, 2017).

Speech Therapy: Speech-language pathologists are professionals who are educated to assess speech and language development and to treat speech and language disorders as well as swallowing disorders. These professionals may implement a variety of interventions to help autistic children improve speech and language.

Occupational Therapy: Common occupational therapy interventions include helping autistic children participate fully in school and social situations, address sensory struggles, and regain skills after injury. Occupational therapy services may include comprehensive evaluations of the client's home and other environments (e.g., workplace, school), recommendations for adaptive equipment and training in its use, and guidance and education for family members and caregivers. Occupational therapy practitioners have a holistic perspective, in which the focus is on adapting the environment to fit the person, and the person is an integral part of the therapy team (The American Occupational Therapy Association, 2021).

Music Therapy: The American Music Therapy Association (2021) describes music therapy as the process in which music is used within a therapeutic relationship to address physical, emotional, cognitive, and social needs of individuals. After assessing the strengths and needs of each client, the qualified music therapist provides the indicated therapy including creating, singing, moving to, and/or listening to music. Through musical involvement in the therapeutic context, clients' abilities are strengthened and transferred to other areas of their lives. Music therapists work with autistic children to activate the whole brain and improve communication behavior and interactions with others.

Possible Needs

An autistic child or teen could have any number of needs just as a neurotypical child could. The needs the child has would determine what, if any, therapy would be beneficial. The following are possible needs that may warrant seeing an affirming therapist.

UNDERSTANDING AUTISM

Communication: Autistic children and teens will vary in their communication strengths and needs. Some children will present as non-verbal or non-speaking. Other children may possess a large vocabulary but lack ability to connect words verbally to their emotions. Some communication needs may warrant seeing a speech therapist.

Writing and other academic needs: Autistic children tend to have an aversion to writing; they may prefer to listen to, watch, or do instead of writing (Attwood & Garnett, 2013). Autistic children may prefer using a keyboard and seem to be more successful when allowed to do so. There may be other academic issues as the autistic child may have learning styles that are not supported in their academic setting. This may require a therapist to help with advocacy needs.

Executive functioning: This can include receptive and expressive language. There can be a large discrepancy between receptive and expressive language ability. Receptive language ability refers to the child's ability to take in or receive language. A child with receptive language issues will likely not hear or process important pieces of information that are being communicated to them verbally. Executive functioning needs can also include processing differences, different and preferred learning styles, and focus/attention differences.

Play: Autistic children may have strong play preferences and interests and are not interested in or possibly not aware of other types of play such as pretend or imaginary play and peer or group play. Many autistic children desire to participate and interact with other peers in group play but may lack the strategies to interact successfully and find the experience to be too overwhelming.

Trauma: Autistic children are vulnerable to experiencing trauma just as much as any child. Some autistic children experience trauma *because* they are autistic—situations, environments, and therapies that are not affirming can create a trauma response for the child.

Phobias and anxiety: Anxiety struggles can be present for some autistic children and teens, and those individuals may need help deescalating their anxiety. There may also be phobias and specific fears that can become debilitating.

Generalization: Some autistic children may struggle with generalizing information. A child may have an awareness in one context and have a difficult time generalizing the information to another context. There may be struggles with understanding nuance, learning through concepts, understanding generalities, discerning *it-depends* situations, and pulling from an existing knowledge base to apply to new or unfamiliar scenarios.

Perspective: Autistic children and teens may be very literal in their thinking (which can be a strength) and find it difficult to consider alternatives or to accept when things are not how they expected or believed they should be. It might be difficult for children to think ahead and to guess what is going to happen next, which means they may become anxious or confused in some situations, especially new situations.

Fear of making mistakes: Some autistic children and teens are prone to developing an almost pathological fear of failing or making errors or mistakes. This fear may cause children to be resistant to trying new experiences or participating in new or unfamiliar events.

Regulation struggles: Many things can create dysregulation challenges for autistic children and teens (Grant, 2017). Some children may struggle with understanding regulation and may need help learning how to regulate their system. This may come in the form of co-regulation work with a therapist or learning coping skills to navigate dysregulating experiences.

Parent and child relationship issues: Some families will enter therapy because there is a strain in the relationship between the child and parent. The strain can be creating an unhealthy home environment and creating additional issues for both the child and parent.

Social navigation: Autistic children and teens typically desire to have friendships, interact with other peers, and participate in social navigation. Many attempts at some type of interaction are met with rejection and anxiety for the autistic child as differences are not readily accepted or appreciated (Grant 2017). Social needs will vary and should be focused on the child, the child's voice should be heard regarding needs and preferences, and special consideration should be taken to avoid trying to change the child or force them to look like a neurotypical accepted presentation.

Self-understanding (appreciation): Many autistic children are not exposed to affirming people or environments. Often, they struggle with conceptualizing their identity as an autistic person. There can be feelings of shame, low self-worth, and internalized ableism. Autistic children may need therapy help to learn value and appreciation for their autistic identity.

Self-advocacy: Milestones Autism Resources (2021) describes self-advocacy as an individual's ability to effectively communicate, convey, negotiate, or assert their own interests, desires, needs, and rights. It involves making informed decisions and taking responsibility for those decisions. Self-knowledge is the first step towards self-advocacy.

An autistic child must know their strengths, needs, and interests before they can begin to advocate. Self-advocacy skills will vary greatly in terms of preference and need but should be learned as early as possible. This begins by learning how to make personal choices, such as making choices about what to eat, how to spend one's free time, and what to do after graduating from high school. The Milestones Autism website lists several self-advocacy skills by age that autistic children and teens could consider and possibly seek therapy help to conceptualize (httwww.milestones.org/).

Grant (2017) put forth the following list regarding possible needs an autistic child might attend mental health therapy to address:
- emotion identification and modulation,
- anxiety and high levels of dysregulation,
- struggling with life transitions, changes to their schedule or routine, new people or experiences, a parent's divorce, or grief issues,
- sensory processing issues in one or multiple areas regarding the eight senses,
- experiencing being bullied at school and in peer situations,
- engaging in unsafe behavior and not understanding safety issues, and
- low self-esteem/worth and needing help to understand autism.

Professionals and parents can be instrumental in providing and accessing services and supports that help children and teens manage their mental health needs. Miller and Smith (2014) stated that autistic children and teens are often bright and capable in many areas, but professionals and parents must be prepared to address any mental health needs that manifest.

A Focus on Strengths

Focusing on the strengths a child possesses, building upon their strengths, and using them to address therapy needs can be an effective and neurodiversity affirming approach for helping autistic children. Stoerkel (2021) proposed that a strengths-based approach is successful because the client is the agent of change by providing the right environment for controlling change. This approach is highly dependent on the thought process and emotional and information processing of the individual. It allows for open communication and thought process for individuals to identify value and assemble their strengths and capacities in the course of change. A strengths-based approach allows for habitable conditions for a person to see themselves at their best, to see the value they bring, by just being themselves.

Pattoni (2012) described a strengths-based practice as a collaborative process between the person supported by services and those supporting them, allowing them to work together to determine an outcome that draws on the person's strengths and assets. In therapeutic settings, it focuses principally on the quality of the relationship that develops between the therapist and the child, as well as the already developed resources the child brings to the process. Working in a collaborative way promotes the opportunity for children to be participants in creating support rather than being directed by the therapist. Strengths-based approaches concentrate on the inherent strengths of children, families, groups, and organizations, deploying personal strengths to aid growth and healing. In essence, to focus on health and well-being is to embrace an asset-based approach where the goal is to promote the positive. Strengths-based approaches value the capacity, skills, knowledge, connections, and potential in children.

A strengths-based approach not only examines the child but also the child's environment. For example, it looks at how systems are set up, especially where power can be out of balance between a system or service and the child it is supposed to serve. In addition, strengths-based approaches identify any constraints that might be holding back an individual's growth. These constraints can be when the individual must deal with social, personal, and/or cultural issues in environments that cannot be balanced fairly (Stoerkel, 2021).

Focusing on strengths and implementing a strengths-based approach does not mean ignoring challenges or needs the child might have or suggesting struggles are strengths. Professionals and parents working from a strength approach will need to work with the child in collaboration—helping them to implement their strengths to successfully address their challenges or needs. In this way, children become co-change agents (partners) in their therapy goals.

UNDERSTANDING AUTISM

Consider the following in the practical application of looking at and utilizing strengths:
- What does the child do well (dresses themself, is kind to others)?
- What has the child accomplished (beat several video games, learned how to use a tablet)?
- How can you assess strengths (inventories, observations, asking the child)?
- What can you observe about strengths the child has (plays independently, follows rules, helps clean the playroom)?

These considerations begin to inform the therapist about the child's strengths and conceptualizing how the strengths can be used to address any therapy needs. It also helps the child recognize they are much more than their therapy needs.

Living Autistic in a Non-Autistic World

Autistic author Naoki Higashida in his book *The Reason I Jump* (2013) writes about being asked if he would like to be "normal." The following response from his book highlights the stigmatization and ableist views that so often impede the autistic individual's advancement through their life journey.

Question: Would you like to be "normal?"

Response: What would we do if there was some way that we could be "normal"? Well, I bet the people around us—our parents and teachers—would be ecstatic with joy and say, "Hallelujah! We'll change them back to normal right now!" And for ages and ages I badly wanted to be normal, too. Living with special needs is so depressing and so relentless; I used to think it would be the best thing if I could just live my life like a normal person

By now, even if somebody developed a medicine to cure autism, I might well choose to stay as I am. Why have I come around to thinking this way?

To give the short version, I've learned that every human being, with or without, needs to strive to do their best, and by striving for happiness you will arrive at happiness. For us, you see, having autism is normal—see we can't know for sure what your "normal" is even like. But so long as we can learn to love ourselves, I'm not sure how much it matters whether we're normal or autistic. (p. 45)

Life as an autistic person does not have a singular look, feel, or experience. Just as the spectrum manifests many different *looks* of autism, so life as an autistic person can look many different ways. Autistic author Dr. Stephen Shore has famously coined "If you have met one child with autism, then you have met one child with autism."

The following is a summary of several constructs that have challenged many of the autistic clients I have worked with over the past two decades. These are important for professionals and parents to consider in their work with autistic children.

A systemic issue: Ableist practices and non-affirming processes in autism are a systemic issue. The myriad of ways that an autistic child can be negatively affected weave throughout home life, extended family, school environment, community, job environment, policies, and laws. When working with autistic children, it is critical to remember how encompassing daily life can become. Everywhere the child goes, whether it be school, interacting with their family, or participating in a community event—they are likely to encounter environments that are not supportive, affirming, or understanding.

School challenge: From the very beginnings of daycare and preschool and throughout college completion, autistic individuals face an uphill battle in most educational settings. The school setting can present some of the greatest challenges to an autistic child. The social and communication demands, rigid learning expectations, processing requirements, and sensory experiences present in every school day can create great dysregulation for autistic children. Many schools find themselves in inadequate positions or are unwilling to provide resources that autistic children need to be their most successful. Professionals and parents can be beneficial in helping to educate school personnel about autism and providing suggestions for services and resources to facilitate a more successful learning experience.

Autism in the family: A diagnosis of autism influences the whole family. The immediate and extended family either can be great support or can create problems for the autistic child. Many of my autistic clients have reported some of their biggest challenges have resulted from judgmental and unaware family members. Parents can help their family by informing extended family about autism and highlighting strengths and affirming approaches.

Therapies and interventions: The intensity and duration of therapy and interventions that an autistic person participates in will vary, but it is likely that most individuals will participate in some form of therapy or intervention sometime during their lifetime. Some individuals may enter and exit therapies and interventions as needed and some may never be involved in therapy. Therapies and interventions may cover a variety of needs depending on the individual. Unfortunately, therapies can create overload for the autistic child (especially if participating in several at once). Further, some therapies have been harmful for autistic children and have created a trauma response. Listening to adult autistic voices is critical in evaluating and navigating affirming therapy practices.

Self-acceptance: Autistic individuals may be in a continuous process of understanding themselves, their diagnosis, how it impacts the world around them, and how the world around them can create support or barriers. Gaining self-awareness of these issues will be critical for the autistic individual to live their most independent and content life. Children around the late elementary and pre-teen years can begin to learn more about their diagnosis and their identity. As they grow and mature, they should master self-advocacy skills and become the best expert on themselves. Professionals and parents can be instrumental in introducing autism to children and assisting them in the self-awareness journey.

Educating others: Autistic individuals may find much of their time spent educating others about autism. Although education and awareness initiatives continue to increase, there still exits much inaccurate information, ignorance, and stereotypes regarding autism. Unfortunately, some autistic individuals have found it easier not to disclose to others that they are autistic because of the mislabeling and stigmatization that can occur. Inevitably, autistics will find themselves in situations where it will be necessary to educate those around them. Resources such as this workbook is a good place to begin to help children learn about autism, which will increase their ability to better educate others. There are also many autistic adults who are writing, teaching, presenting, and sharing information that can be helpful in educating others. Resources by actual autistics can be found in the appendix section of this workbook.

Listening to Autistic Voices: Anastasia Phelps

Anastasia Phelps is an autistic 18-year-old spoken word and expressive artist. Among her many activities, she dedicates herself to advocating for those who are neurodivergent through public speaking, writing, and expressive arts. In her spoken word (*Fearfully and Wonderfully Made*), she shares some of her perspective and feelings about navigating her world as an autistic teen. *Fearfully and Wonderfully Made* was the first spoken word Anastasia created when she was 14 years old. She then began speaking publicly and entered her spoken word in competitions which lead to competing in a national competition in which she placed 5th overall. More about Anastasia can be found on her Facebook page, Beautiful Not Broken.

Fearfully and Wonderfully Made
You're not good enough
You're inadequate
Useless, Worthless
They don't want you
They never will

You are right to question
Your instincts and decisions
Because you know that you
will always say and do the wrong thing

You don't fit in
Don't even dream of being one of them
You're always going to be on the outside
Desperately trying to get in

My head spins in an endless cyclone
Of anger, embarrassment, guilt, regret
Like a house divided against itself that cannot stand

UNDERSTANDING AUTISM

Crumbling

The lies and labels of the enemy,
They fracture my thoughts and self-esteem

Yet I have been told
In God's own words
that I am fearfully and wonderfully made

And there is a difference between
What I tell myself, what the world tells me,
And who God has created me to be

Autism, Asperger's, brain abnormalities,
Short-term memory loss, ADHD
Why do you label me?

Overwhelmed, overstimulated, overlooked,
Shy, painfully awkward, annoying,
Brainless, melting-down, misjudged...
Broken

Don't be noticed, just blend in
Be sure to speak to me slowly,
So maybe I'll understand
Be sure to change your tone,
Like I am an infant unable to comprehend

You try to paint my portrait
With your brush of judgement
Pulling me into what you think
My definition of normal should be

But haven't you heard?
The Bible tells me that
I am fearfully and wonderful made
And there's the difference between
What I tell myself, what the world tells me,
And who God has created me to be!

Though the world calls me "retarded,"
God calls me chosen, child
Knitted together in the womb of my mother

By the One who created the very brush you use to define me

You see, I was made in God's image
My story was written before I was formed
He knows the number of hairs on my head
And He tells me
"Do not be afraid,"

I will not be afraid because
His eye is on the sparrow,
And I know He watches over me

And I am fearfully and wonderfully made

Listening To Autistic Voices: Kyle Calderon

Kyle Calderon is an autistic adult and Licensed Master Social Worker in New York state. He obtained a master's degree in social work from Fordham University in 2017, during which he completed his internship at an agency providing advocacy for autistic adults and education to the support staff. He now provides therapy for individuals of all ages and families, with a focus on neurodivergent and transgender individuals. He also provides trainings on affirming care for both populations. He is currently collecting hours for independent licensure and is on track to obtain the Registered Play Therapist credential as well. In the following, Kyle shares some of his experiences being autistic.

When I was told I had Asperger Syndrome in 2004, I had mixed feelings. While it gave me a reason to understand things about myself, new pressures manifested to change who I was. After my diagnosis, there were more focused directives from others such as I need to work on eye contact or socialize more or in specific ways. I was fortunate enough to avoid being put through applied behavior analysis (ABA) and any non-affirming "treatments," but I could not avoid absorbing the shame that comes from not meeting people's expectations and being told how I presented myself is a problem.

When I was 15, I participated in a social skills group with other autistic youth. I did not mind it, since it gave me something to do, and the therapists were nice. I stopped going after a year and forgot about the group until I was in my introduction to social work course five years later. My fieldwork placement ended up being that same group and same therapist. At that time, I thought I did not know anything about autism, as I had been told autism and Asperger's were vastly different in presentation. While the therapist mentioned that the teen groups ran smoothly other than some side chatter, the younger groups were more of a challenge. We struggled trying to get the younger children to act "appropriately" in group, which I now look back on and realize was like trying to put a square peg in a round hole. I feel a bit of sadness when I think of one boy, who appeared to be in distress when the staff tried to get him to participate.

I discovered neurodiversity and the social model of disability while I was in graduate school in 2016. This changed my life and my understanding of autism completely. I learned about this concept from autistic adults sharing their experiences on social media. I started to move away from the Asperger's label and identify as autistic. I had previously not called myself autistic, because I thought I could not; I thought I was "on the spectrum" but not really autistic. I had learned, however, that it was not a word to be ashamed of, and I did not want to participate in a "I'm not like those people over there" type of mentality. While it was freeing to know that there was a community of people like me that embraced their autistic traits, I also felt shame that came with being different in a world that was not designed for people like me.

During my graduate school internship, I worked with intellectually and developmentally disabled adults; and I was celebrated for my strength-based approach, lived experience, and education on the social model of disability. For the first time, I felt empowered to help the autistic individuals feel understood. Unfortunately, I could not stay there after graduation and had to start looking elsewhere to further my career.

My sister (who is not autistic but is a speech-language pathologist) is as passionate about neurodiversity as I am and suggested I go into the field of behaviorism in order to change the field and their perspectives; but I knew my limits and that it would be too triggering for me to go into a field that goes against everything I believe in and have to advocate from the bottom up. Now that I knew the other side (the neurodiversity affirming side), I could not go back; I went as far as cancelling job interviews when I learned they involved non-affirming practices. While I had to be less picky with jobs in the beginning, I was determined to eventually open my own private practice to provide neurodiversity-affirming care.

In my first role as a therapist in 2019, I was required to sit through a presentation on autism by an ABA therapist. I remember the pain I felt throughout this presentation, particularly as this therapist called the lining up of toys "inappropriate," and shamed stimming when there were no safety concerns. I often felt alone, and I over compensated, because if I was honest about my flaws, I was proving that people like me do not belong in this field. I knew about how being autistic gave me my strengths of empathy, being less judgmental, and overall dedication to my work, but the world that was not aware of neurodiversity would not see it that way. Despite my best efforts, the internalized ableism of trying to be exceptional *despite* being autistic was ingrained in me.

I finally felt at home in 2020 when I discovered other neurodiversity-affirming specialists online; there was a community of people like me who specialized in working with this population in a manner that is understanding and does not try to change autistic individuals. I have learned much since connecting with others in this network. When operating under the neurodiversity-affirming paradigm, being autistic is not a reason to seek therapy; rather, reasons for seeking therapy include addressing sensory issues, learning communication skills, learning self-advocacy, and treating mental health concerns that come from experiencing intense emotions and minority stress. I continue to seek training and consultation from like-minded individuals so I can advance and not feel isolated.

Autistic individuals have a variety of needs just like anyone else. Some children have difficulty at both home and school; others may manage at school because they have learned how to mask but may have trouble regulating themselves at home. The autistic children and teens I work with often do well when I allow them to take the lead and choose an activity (a more nondirective approach). I have also worked with youth that experience anxiety from a nondirective approach. They seem to struggle with not knowing what to do or talk about and are more engaged and relieved when I lead the session with a game, workbook, or expressive activity. The youth I work with may have experienced trauma from being secluded and/or restrained at school, bullying, and being put through behaviorist interventions that shamed them for being themselves. Therefore, my goal is to give them a safe space where their stimming, sharing of special interests, and otherwise expressing themselves is welcome. I provide psychoeducation to parents on autism and how to support their child, educate them on how to find appropriate resources, and emphasize their child's strengths. When and how I self-disclose being autistic varies, but when I do, parents have communicated to me I give them hope for their child's future, and the youth are often surprised to meet an adult like themself.

Among the autistic adults I work with, common issues include vocational issues; shame related to not being understood by others; and issues related to intersectionality of race, culture, and/or gender. A large overlap has been identified between the autistic and transgender community, another population I work with frequently. Assigned-female-at-birth individuals tend to be less likely to receive a diagnosis due to gender-based stereotypes (Gratton and Cheaney, 2020). Suicidal ideation among autistic adults has been found to be as high as 66% in one study (Cassidy et. al, 2014), with unemployment and underemployment rates at 39% (Ohl et.al, 2017). A correlation between Post Traumatic Stress Disorder and autism has also been observed (Huravi-Lamden et al, 2018). I personally believe that these statistics start from a young age, when children are constantly forced to mask who they are.

By the time the adults I work with have come to me, they have experienced years, if not decades, of trauma, abuse, bullying, shame, and low self-worth. Many of them did not know they were autistic until later in life. While some are more optimistic about the therapy process than others, they usually are relieved they do not have to educate me on autism or their lived experience. I make it my mission to give my adult clients the support and strength-based point of view that they should have received in the past. If they have been recently diagnosed, I may congratulate them for finally getting the answer they needed. My hope is that neurodiversity-affirming care will continue to expand, so individuals can know their strengths, and society can be prepared to support them, from an early age. I believe the best way to do this is for clinicians to listen to autistic adults.

Valuing the Autistic Child

When working with autistic children and teens, it is critical for professionals to assess and conceptualize each individual child to fully understand the particular child's strengths and needs. Although there may be some commonalities, each autistic child will present with their uniqueness. Professionals are encouraged to develop a process to help them build a relationship with the child, get to know the individual child, and more accurately identify the child's strengths and needs, as well as any particulars a child might be experiencing related to being autistic. This process can be accomplished through parent-completed inventories, background information from the child's parents, professional observations, and simply talking with and spending time with the child. Grant (2017) developed a formal assessment process in AutPlay® Therapy that involves conducting a play observation of the child with the professional in a playroom, observing the parent and child playing together, and having the parent complete inventories to identify strengths and needs of the child.

Any type of therapy, support, care, or education process with an autistic child or teen should be grounded in valuing the child's identity. Professionals and parents will want to conceptualize how their interactions with the child promote value and acceptance and avoid ableist concepts. Lambert (2018) stated that non-autistic disability advocates often neglect to apply the social model when they talk about autism and proposed five suggestions for valuing autistic individuals:

1. ***Nothing About Us, Without Us:*** A popular adage with disability advocates—and it's still relevant. You can't talk about autism if you're ignoring autistic people and what we have to say. All those people advocating for a cure? Most of them aren't autistic.
2. ***You Don't Know Me:*** Much of the information out there about autism isn't accurate to the real experiences of autistic people. It's nice to hear that you're interested in our issues, but don't assume you know more about autism than we do. In fact, it's sometimes best to assume that you don't know anything about autism at all.
3. ***Educate Yourself:*** So maybe you don't know anything about autism. It's time to learn—from us. Read what autistic activists write about our experiences—not only the voices that are easy to find, but also those that are often quieter. Autistic women, autistic people of color, queer and trans autistic people, and poor autistic people all have stories to tell.
4. ***This Space Is Our Space:*** Your disability-centered social circles, articles, and theories aren't always accessible to autistic people, even though we are just as disabled as you. If you don't make any efforts to make easy-read materials, sensory-friendly environments, or spaces where people can communicate in the ways that are most comfortable for them, you aren't including us.

5. **Who Are You Speaking To?:** Many autistic advocates prefer *identity-first* language ("autistic person" instead of "person with autism"). Our disability is part of us, and we don't want to dance around it. And please—don't call us *high functioning* or *low functioning*. If you don't respect our language, you don't respect us. (paras. 6–10)

Grant et al. (2021) proposes a guideline for being autism friendly that includes several philosophical points neurotypical individuals can implement to provide value and affirmation for autistic children:
1. Do not assume the autistic child has limitations. Half of those with a formal diagnosis of autism have average or above-average intelligence.
2. Ask the child about autism and listen to what they say.
3. Remember that processing speed and communication might be different from your own and differences are valued as okay.
4. Remember social interactions may look differently. This is not negative; it is different but not a lesser way of doing things.
5. Do not rely on nonverbal messages or body language to communicate to an autistic child. Be clear, with no passive-aggressive behavior.
6. Respect the child's right to decide how they want or do not want to talk about autism and how they want autism referenced.
7. Talk to the autistic child and ask them what they are thinking and feeling; do not assume based on their body language and behavior.
8. Use visual supports (schedules, pictures) when relaying information. Do not communicate only verbally.
9. Do not judge behavior that is different from your own.
10. Look for the strengths the autistic child possesses and try to build upon those strengths.
11. See the world from the child's viewpoint. How are they experiencing what is happening?
12. Do not try to force the child to be like, look like, and act like you. Respect and learn about neurodiversity.

Essentially, the concept of valuing a child is not complicated. The professional or parent can simply reflect on how they would want to be treated by a professional they might be seeing. Would they want to be heard, be listened to, have a say in what happens to them, be able to freely share and ask questions, make decisions concerning what happens to them, etc.? In most cases, adults would answer yes to all the above questions and desire this type of value. We should do no less for the children and teens we work with and serve. Value empowers, and empowerment can achieve and heal as this becomes the meaningful pursuit in our work with the autistic population.

How to Use This Guidebook

Autistic children and teens could have various needs that require addressing, but one central issue that is often neglected is helping autistic children and teens understand autism from an affirming, strengths-based perspective. Many children lack an appropriate awareness of autism and may lack the ability to process their thoughts and emotions regarding having an autism diagnosis.

This guidebook is designed to help autistic children learn about their diagnosis and process through their thoughts, feelings, and questions about autism. It also is designed to assist both professionals and parents in helping children and teens understand autism and process through their thoughts and emotions about being autistic. Parents may share this guidebook with family members and other individuals such as school staff, recreational workers, church staff, etc. who may interact regularly with their child to help these individuals better understand an autistic child.

Professionals and parents are encouraged to learn more about autism. The resources section of this guidebook lists several books, websites, apps, and games that can help professionals and parents gain insight about autism and can provide additional tools to help children and teens explore more information.

This guidebook can be completed by starting at the beginning and going through each worksheet/activity with the child, or each page (worksheet) can be targeted separately as an individual concept to explain and explore with the child. Each worksheet provides an opportunity for the child to share their thoughts and questions and for professionals and parents to answer the child's questions and further explain concepts related to autism.

Although many professionals and parents may be well educated about autism, much of the information has historically been presented through a medical model (ableist) lens. This guidebook will help professionals and parents understand how to be neurodiversity affirming, valuing, strength-based, and supportive of the autistic child. Information is presented to aid professionals and parents in sharing and processing through each worksheet page/topic. Each worksheet includes suggestions on how to use the worksheet and information that can be shared and discussed for optimal results.

The Worksheets

UNDERSTANDING AUTISM

Using and Processing the Worksheet

This Worksheet Is Designed to Help You Understand Yourself and Autism

This section contains two worksheets designed to be introductory worksheets that explain to the child or teen that we are going to be using this workbook to discuss autism. On one worksheet, the child/teen is asked to draw a picture of themselves doing something fun. The child may draw more than one thing that they like to do for fun. This activity is designed to be fun for the child and to endear them to the workbook. The drawing of the picture can also provide insight for the professional or parent to better understand what the child/teen likes to do for fun. Identifying what the child likes to do for fun provides opportunity for the professional or parent to utilize this information and engage with the child in the fun activities they like and possibly use the fun activities as a motivation for completing worksheet directives.

Professionals and parents are encouraged to have a variety of materials available for drawing the picture—pencils, markers, paints, etc.—and allow the child to choose the material they are comfortable using. Children/teens should be instructed that the drawing of the picture is for fun, and they can be as creative as they want in completing the picture.

The second worksheet asks the child/teen to list three things they believe they do well. This worksheet introduces a continual theme throughout the workbook of focusing on strengths and helping the child/teen focus on improving their self-worth while learning about autism. Some autistic children may struggle with self-worth issues and may have difficulty identifying things they believe they do well. This provides insight for the professional or parent to better understand the autistic child and the social and emotional challenges the child may be facing.

UNDERSTANDING AUTISM

This Worksheet Is Designed to Help You Understand Yourself Better

Let's start by drawing a picture of you doing something fun.

UNDERSTANDING AUTISM

This Worksheet Is Also Designed to Help You Understand Autism

Let's learn a little bit more about you. List three things you believe you do well.

1) _____

2) _____

3) _____

UNDERSTANDING AUTISM

Using and Processing the Worksheet

What Does Autism Mean?

The importance of these worksheets is to help children and teens have an accurate definition that they can understand and make sure there are no misunderstood beliefs. For some children and teens, this may be the first time they are hearing the terminology of autism or the first time they are fully exploring what it means. There are three worksheets: the first is a blank picture image, the second is a list of words that can be checked off, and the third has the word *autism* written in the middle of the page. The professional may choose to use any or all of the worksheets.

The first worksheet page asks the child to draw a picture or write in the blank image what they think autism means. This provides the child or teen opportunity to draw their thoughts about autism or write what they think autism means. If the child cannot or does not what to draw or write, they can say what they think, and the professional or parent can write it down. The child or teen may express one or several thoughts or they may not have any thoughts. The professional or parent should give the child or teen the opportunity to complete this page before the professional or parent begins to explain what autism means. It is important to understand what the child or teen believes before processing any additional information.

The second worksheet page has the child put a check by the words that they think describe an autistic person. This gives the child or teen a more concrete way to identify and express what they think about autism and can reveal any inaccuracies the child may have about autism. It is important to address inaccuracies that the child or teen presents and help them understand accurate descriptors and information about autism. The third worksheet lets the child draw or write whatever comes to mind when they hear the word autism.

A comprehensive resource for professionals and parents is available from the Autism Self Advocacy Network (ASAN), which provides several resources for explaining autism and includes a parent guide (https://autisticadvocacy.org/).

UNDERSTANDING AUTISM

What Does Autism Mean?

Draw a picture or write in the screen below what you think autism means.

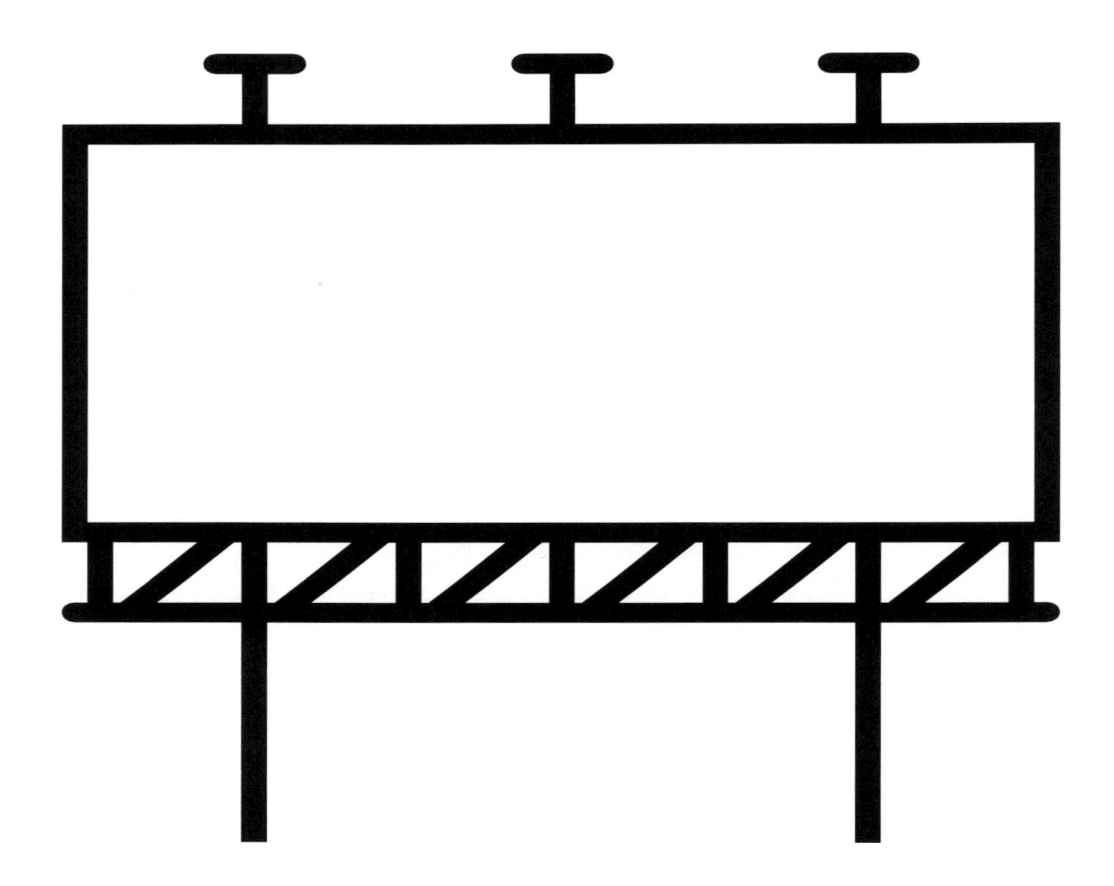

UNDERSTANDING AUTISM

What Does Autism Mean?

Put a check by all the words below that you think describe an autistic person.

__Smart   __Sad   __Talented

__Popular   __Lonely

__Friendly   __Angry   __Loner

__Social Problems   __Shy

__Fun   __Creative   __Athletic

__Scared   __No Friends

__Aggressive   __Happy   __Weird

__Confident   __Nice

__Cool   __Not Cool   __Gifted

UNDERSTANDING AUTISM

What Does Autism Mean?

Talk about, draw, or write anything you want on this page that you think of when you hear the word autism.

AUTISM

UNDERSTANDING AUTISM

Using and Processing the Worksheet

What Are Some of Your Questions About Autism?

Many children/teens have questions about autism. This worksheet page instructing to write in the thought bubbles some of your questions about autism, gives the child or teen the opportunity to write down some of their questions. If the child or teen is not able to write, they can say what their questions are and the professional or parent can write the questions down. Typically, children and teens will have some questions about autism. Some children may begin by asking "What is autism?" The questions will likely vary from generic to more specific. The professional or parent should address the child's questions as accurately as possible. If the professional or parent is not sure what the answer is, they can tell the child or teen they can research the question and discover the answer together.

Regarding autism, there are many questions that do not have definitive answers. If the professional or parent encounters this situation, they should explain to the child or teen that there is currently not one specific answer for their questions and try to provide the child or teen with as much information as is possible. The professional or parent should encourage the child or teen to ask questions anytime they feel unsure or confused about autism.

Some helpful book resources are listed below:
Sincerely Your Autistic Child: What People on the Autism Spectrum Wish Their Parents Knew About Growing Up, Acceptance, and Identity by Emily Paige Ballou, Sharon daVanport, and Morenike Giwa Onaiwu.

The Reason I Jump: The Inner Voice of a 13-Year-Old Boy with Autism by Naoki Hogashida.

Stars in Her Eyes: Navigating the Maze of Childhood Autism by Linda Barboa and Elizabeth Obrey

UNDERSTANDING AUTISM

What Are Some of Your Questions About Autism?

Write in the thought bubbles below some of your questions about autism.

UNDERSTANDING AUTISM

Using and Processing the Worksheet

What Are Your Feelings About Being Autistic?

Feelings can be very challenging for autistic children. Repetitive work on identifying and processing feelings of any type, especially those related to how the child/teen feels about autism, is critical. The following three worksheets give the child or teen the opportunity to identify and process their feelings. The worksheet titled "What Are Your Feelings about Being Autistic?" is a guided illustration using a heart symbol to help the child identify what they feel about being autistic. Several common feelings are provided as a guide to help the child more easily select their feelings.

Once the child has completed the coloring activity, the professional or parent can talk with the child about each feeling they identified. Specific focus should be placed on any negative feelings that the child identifies. Helping the child process through their negative feelings may require multiple conversations and/or interventions implemented via therapy.

The worksheet titled "Sometimes Emotions Are Hard to Understand. Let's Practice Understanding Emotions" provides a short story about a situation that would create multiple emotions. There are several follow up questions that ask the child or teen to identify how the character in the story is feeling and how they themselves would feel. This short activity can help the professional or parent better understand the level of emotional awareness and comprehension the child or teen currently possesses. Professionals and parents can easily create additional short stories for further practice.

The third worksheet is a mandala the child can color and notice if they feel calmer or relaxed after coloring the mandala. If the child responds positively to the mandala, they can continue to use mandalas as a coping tool. These worksheets provide a beginning for identifying and processing feelings and can be revisited periodically to assess if the child's feelings have changed. Professionals and parents should be aware that the child's feelings about being autistic may vary from positive to negative depending on what is happening in their environment and the messages they are receiving about autism.

UNDERSTANDING AUTISM

What Are Your Feelings About Being Autistic?

Color in the heart below with your feelings about being autistic. Each color is a different feeling.

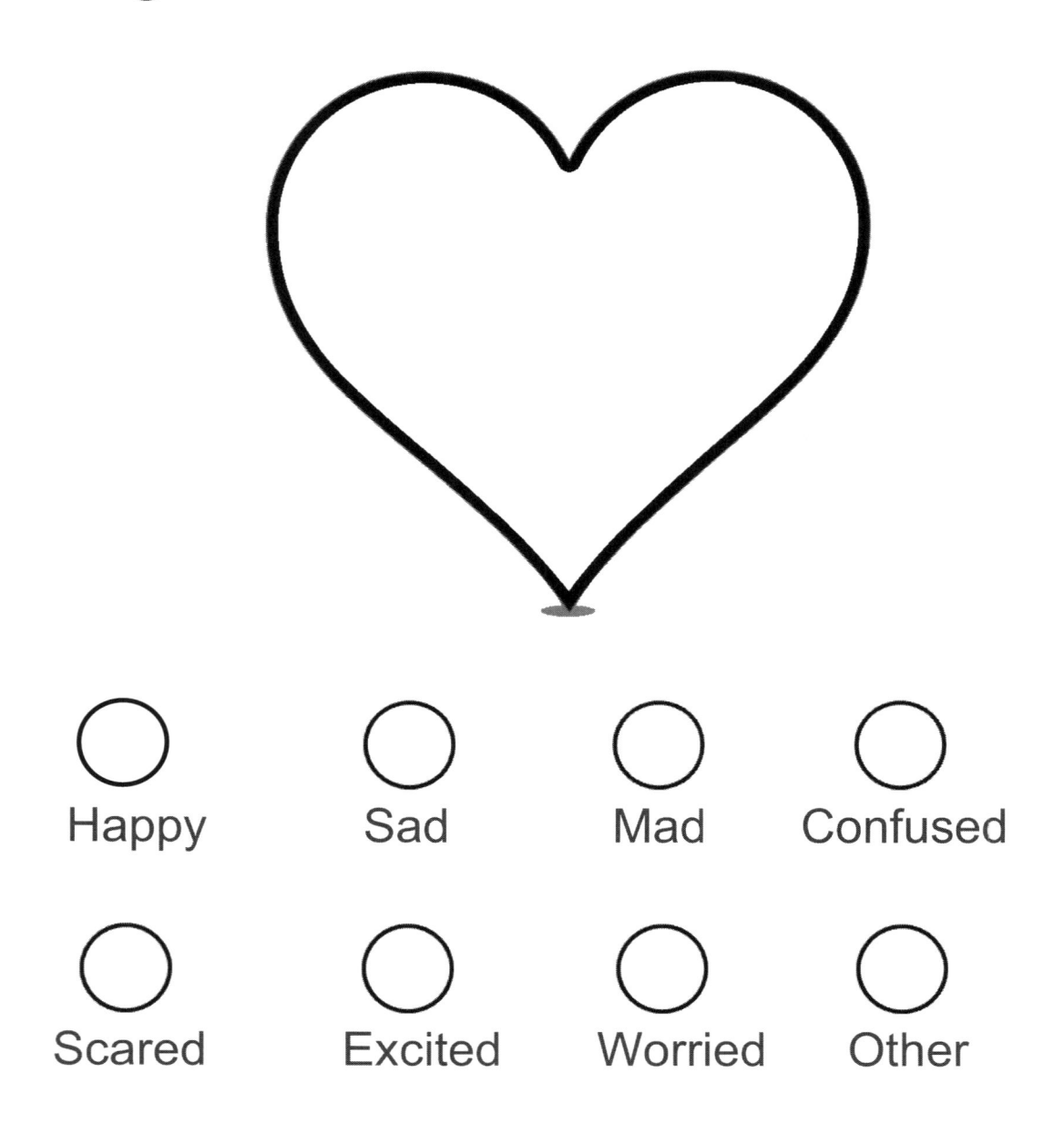

○ Happy   ○ Sad   ○ Mad   ○ Confused

○ Scared   ○ Excited   ○ Worried   ○ Other

UNDERSTANDING AUTISM

Sometimes Emotions Are Hard to Understand. Let's Practice Understanding Emotions.

Read the story below (or have it read to you) and answer the questions.

The Story

You arrive at school one morning and go into your classroom and sit down beside a boy you have talked to before. The boy is crying. The boy tells you that his favorite cat ran out of his house this morning, into the street, and was hit and killed by a car.

The Questions

What do you think this boy is feeling?

How do you know he is feeling this way?

How would you feel if it were your pet?

How would you respond to the boy?

Why would you respond this way?

What would make you uncomfortable about this situation?

What else can you say about feelings and this story?

Sometimes It Is Hard to Feel Calm.

Color in this mandala and notice if it helps you feel calm or relaxed.

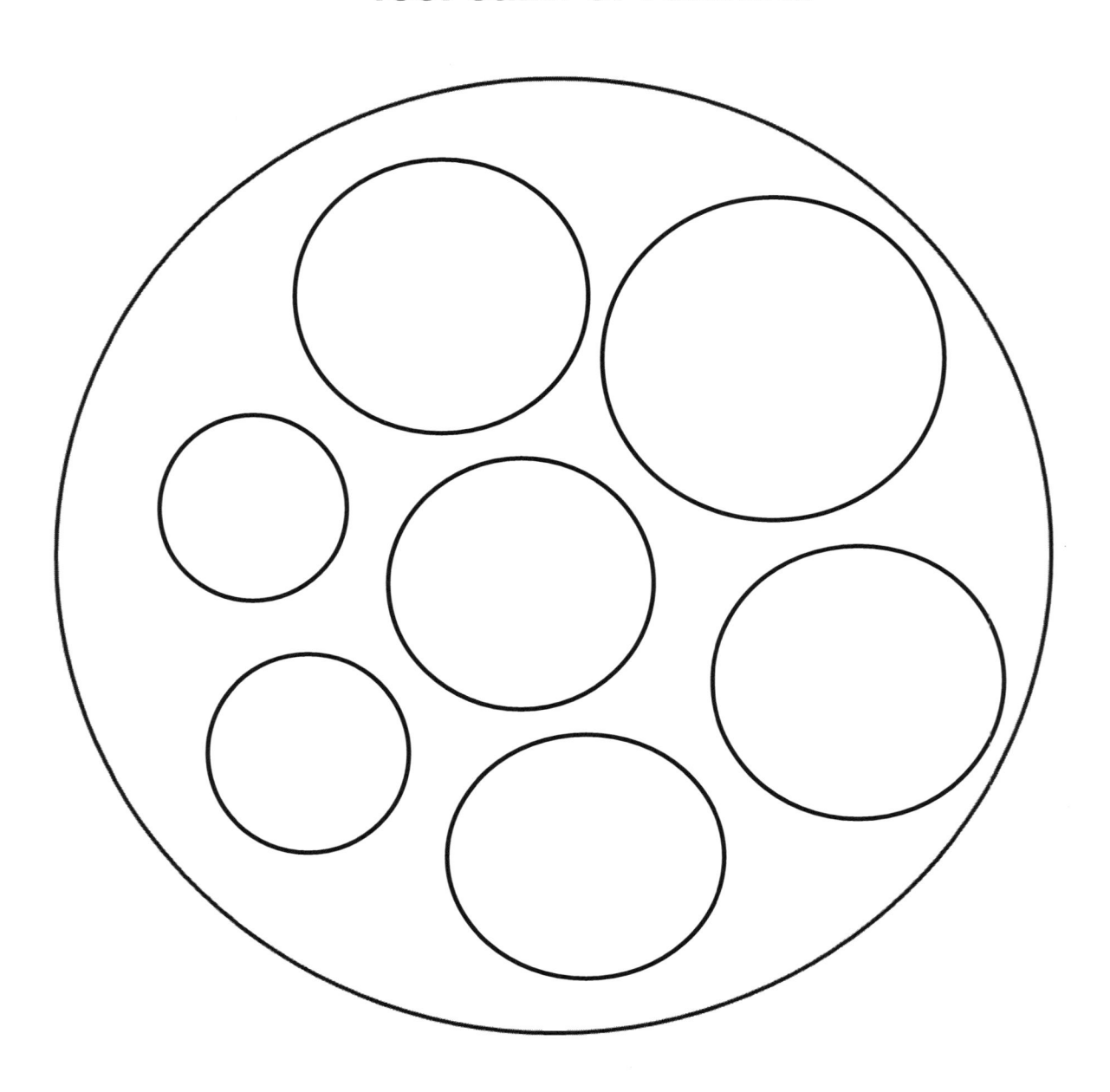

UNDERSTANDING AUTISM

Using and Processing the Worksheet

What Are Some Things That Might Be Part of Being Autistic?

These worksheets provide the opportunity for children and teens to gain a better understanding of characteristics they may possess. The first worksheet asks children to write down characteristics, descriptors, or anything they think describes or is a part of being autistic. If the child does not want to write or cannot write, they can talk about what they think. This worksheet further provides a list of descriptors or traits. The child is instructed to circle anything in the list that they believe describes them. If the child cannot read, the professional or parent can read the list to the child.

The first worksheet is a starting point for helping children conceptualize characteristics that may be a part of themselves. It also helps children and teens discover positive characteristics about autism. Many autistic children need to work on understanding autism, gain perspective on what it means to be an autistic person, and learn how to value the unique characteristics they possess.

The second worksheet asks the child or teen to match a typical term associated with autism to its correct definition. This worksheet helps children begin to put a formal language to their diagnosis and understand what terms that may be a part of them mean. Many children will not be aware of the terms and will need help from the professional or parent in correctly matching the term with its definition. Professionals and parents should process the worksheets with the child or teen to make sure that they understand the characteristics and terms that are a part of their autistic experience, making sure to emphasize and highlight the positive characteristics.

What Are Some Things That Are Part of Being Autistic?

Talk about, draw, or write what you think.

Let's talk about some of the common traits that may go with autism. Circle the ones you think are a part of you.

- I remember things best by seeing pictures.
- Sometimes I feel anxious or worried.
- Loud noises, lights, and things touching my skin bother me.
- Sometimes I have a hard time feeling calm.
- I don't know what to say to other kids.
- I don't always know what I am feeling.
- I like to know what is happening in my day.
- I'm uncomfortable with new situations and people.
- I can focus on things I am interested in.
- I like to play or be by myself.

UNDERSTANDING AUTISM

What Are Some Common Words That Go with Autism?

Let's do some matching. Draw a line from the word to its definition.

WORDS

Stimming

Neurotypical

Regulation

Dysregulation

IEP

Sensory

Perseverating

DEFINITIONS

| A term used to describe someone who does not have autism. |
| Refers to different experiences that a body might have. |
| A thought or action that keeps repeating. |
| A school plan designed to give children things they need at school. |
| Feeling overwhelmed and out of control. |
| Repeating body movements or sounds to help stay calm. |
| Being able to manage and control emotions to stay calm. |

Using and Processing the Worksheet

How Do You Think You Became Autistic? Will You Always Be Autistic?

Autistic children and teens will likely come to a point in their life where they question how they became autistic. This can be a sensitive subject to address as they may have heard several different things about autism from various sources. Leading research initiatives suggest that autism is likely genetic and there may be multiple genes and chromosomes that are impacted, thus most all autistic individuals are born this way. It is appropriate to explain to children that we may not have all the answers, but their being autistic is not bad or wrong.

The first worksheet provides a small section where children can circle what they think about how they became autistic. It is important to make sure that children do not blame themselves or others and view autism as a bad thing. The most appropriate response is "Some people are just autistic."

The second worksheet asks the child or teen to think about and discuss if they will always be autistic. The short answer is yes, but this is another question that may be challenging for the child. Some children may not really be wondering about being autistic but instead wondering about a current specific need they have that they relate to being autistic. Being autistic is something the child will live with on some level the rest of their life, so it is important to keep discussions as positive as possible. The goal is that the child will understand and have an acceptance about autism. Conversations should not stray into the negative or create a situation where the child or teen views autism as a terrible condition. Conversations should be realistic but empowering for the child.

UNDERSTANDING AUTISM

How Do You Think You Became Autistic?

Circle what you think is true below.

How did you become autistic?

I did something bad.

My parents did something bad.

I was born this way.

Some people are just autistic.

I don't know.

Something else.

Let's write down what we know.

_____

_____

_____

UNDERSTANDING AUTISM

Will You Always Be Autistic?

Yes
No
Maybe

Let's write down what we know.
_____
_____
_____
_____
_____
_____
_____
_____

UNDERSTANDING AUTISM

Using and Processing the Worksheet

Do You Know an Autistic Person?

There are many autistic individuals, and often children may know someone in their life who is autistic. These two worksheets provide opportunity for children and teens to understand there are other people who may be similar to themselves, or at least who are also autistic. The first worksheet asks the child or teen to write a person's name who is autistic and draw a picture of the person. The second worksheet asks the child or teen to write some words that describe the person they know who is autistic. If the child cannot write, they can say words and the professional or parent can write the words down.

Once the worksheets have been completed, the professional or parent should ask the child to talk about the person, what the person is like, some of the things the child may like about the person, and some of the positive characteristics of the person. The child may not be able to think of anyone. In this situation, if the professional or parent knows an autistic person that the child knows, the professional or parent can share this with the child, and they can then complete the worksheet about that person. There is a wide variety of autistic individuals. The child may know more than one person and the child may know people at very different need levels than the child. When completing this worksheet, it might be helpful for the professional or parent to be prepared to talk about how another autistic person may be very different from the child and how there is a wide presentation of being autistic.

UNDERSTANDING AUTISM

Do You Know Someone Who Is Autistic? If So, Draw a Picture of Them Below.

Write the Person's Name _____

Draw a Picture of the Person

Do You Know Someone Who Is Autistic? If So, Describe That Person.

Write some words that describe the person.

Using and Processing the Worksheet

What Does Spectrum Mean in Autism Spectrum Disorder?

Autism is a spectrum, meaning there are multiple manifestations of autism sharing the same diagnosis code. This is sometimes a challenging concept for autistic children to understand. Many autistic children are literal thinkers, and they may have a difficult time understanding what the differences are between themselves and another person who manifests elsewhere on the spectrum who looks different from them.

This worksheet is designed to provide a visual image and discussion of the spectrum. Professionals and parents will likely need to explain what spectrum means—that there are autistic people who have several needs, and there are autistic people who have little to no needs. A visual image is often helpful in illustrating this point and helping the child accurately define how they present on the spectrum. The visual on this worksheet illustrates the neurodiversity infinity symbol.

Professionals and parents should help the child define how they present on the spectrum. When completing this worksheet, professionals and parents may want to incorporate the worksheet on strengths located in this workbook. This is an appropriate time to discuss how strengths and needs can influence where a person is on the spectrum.

UNDERSTANDING AUTISM

What Is a Spectrum? How Do You Describe Yourself on the Autism Spectrum?

Let's write about what we know.

_____

_____

_____

_____

_____

UNDERSTANDING AUTISM

Using and Processing the Worksheet

Where You Are on the Spectrum Sometimes Depends on the Strengths and Needs You have. What Strengths Do You Think You Have?

These worksheet pages provide an opportunity for professionals and parents to talk about strengths. Most autistic children and teens can benefit from working on strengths. The worksheet "What Strengths Do You Have?" presents several strengths that the child or teen can color in if they believe they possess the strength. This worksheet can also function as a mini assessment of the child's current strengths. Professionals and parents may also want to complete this worksheet indicating the strengths they believe the child possesses and compare their answers with the child's answers.

The worksheet "What Are Some More Things We Know about You?" provides opportunity for the child or teen to finish some short sentences identifying several things they believe are strengths they possess. If the child cannot write, they can verbalize responses and the professional or parent can write them down.

Most autistic children will have strengths. The professional and parent will want to help the child or teen identify strengths if the child or teen is struggling to think of anything. These worksheets provide an opportunity to encourage the child by discussing the strengths. Autistic children and teens may have experienced many environments where they have been told what is wrong about them. It is vital that children can realize the abilities they have and the strengths they possess.

What Strengths Do You Have?

Color in the circles for each strength that you think you currently have.

○	○	○	○
Making Friends	Talking	Listening	Video Games

○	○	○	○
Art	Sports	Playing with Others	Taking Turns

○	○	○	○
Being in Groups	Going to Stores	Expressing Feelings	Writing

○	○	○	○
___	___	___	___

What Are Some More Things We Know about You?

I'm good at_____

I know a lot about_____

I'm able to_____

I can usually_____

I can do well at_____

I like to_____

I'm smart about_____

I know I can_____

I can accomplish_____

I'm better than most people at_____

People tell me I'm good at_____

UNDERSTANDING AUTISM

Using and Processing the Worksheet

What Needs Do You Think You Have?

On this worksheet page, children and teens are asked to color in the circles corresponding to needs the child or teen believes they could improve upon. It is helpful for the child to share what needs they believe they have. It is fine if the child does not identify any needs, and any needs they do identify should be discussed.

If the child or teen does have any needs, it is important to identify them accurately. The needs may be something that can be addressed in therapy. It is important to help children and teens remain positive about themselves and recognize their strengths while working on needs. It is also important to note that some children may think they have a need that is not a need.

The awareness of real needs a child may have helps professionals and parents work better with the child. Professionals and parents may also want to complete this worksheet identifying what they believe are the child's needs and compare their answers to the child's answers.

UNDERSTANDING AUTISM

What Needs Do You Think You Have?

Color in the circles for any need you think you have.

○	○	○	○
Making Friends	Talking	Listening	Relaxing

○	○	○	○
Video Games	Asking Questions	Writing	Taking Turns

○	○	○	○
Being in Groups	Going to Stores	Expressing Feelings	Eating

○	○	○	○
_____	_____	_____	_____

Using and Processing the Worksheet

Is There Something You Believe You Are Not Good at That You Want to Improve?

There are two worksheets focused on this topic. The first worksheet provides the opportunity for children and teens to express how they feel about working on an improvement. It also includes an instruction to the child or teen to draw a picture of themselves doing something they think they are not currently doing well. This activity helps the child focus positively on improvements and gives them a visual picture of being successful.

The worksheet "Let's Write a List of Some of the Ways You Could Work on What You Want to Improve" provides opportunity to list several ideas for how to work on improvement. The professional or parent should allow the child or teen to think of anything they can first and then assist with additional ideas.

Professionals and parents should make sure that children understand they can improve upon anything that is important to them. Professionals and parents should be affirming in helping children improve any areas they identify, being mindful that it is something important to the child and not something someone has told the child that they need to change about themselves.

UNDERSTANDING AUTISM

Is There Something You Believe You Are Not Good at That You Want to Improve?

Talk about, draw, or write what you think.

Draw a picture of yourself doing something that you want to improve.

UNDERSTANDING AUTISM

Let's Write a List of Some of the Ways You Could Work on What You Want to Improve.

How about _____

This is a way _____

Maybe this _____

Try this _____

Another way _____

Or this _____

And maybe _____

Also _____

UNDERSTANDING AUTISM

Using and Processing the Worksheet

Do You Think Being Autistic Is Good, Bad, or You're Not Sure?

This is a self-reflective worksheet page where the child or teen is simply instructed to identify if they think being autistic is good, bad, or not sure. It is important for professionals and parents to understand how a child views being autistic. Once the child has chosen what they think, professionals or parents should discuss with the child why they think this way. If the child indicates they believe it is bad or they are not sure, professionals and parents should ask the child to explain why they believe it is bad or why they feel unsure. Regardless of how the child responds, professionals and parents should try to convey to the child affirming and positive sentiments about being autistic.

Some of the noted benefits that autistic individuals possess include the following:

- rarely judge others,
- rarely lie,
- not tied to social expectations,
- logical,
- interesting,
- have good memories,
- unique creative views,
- less materialistic,
- free of prejudice,
- passionate, and
- can focus on certain interests for long periods of time.

Ultimately it is critical that children have a healthy view of self. Helping an autistic child learn acceptance and possess a positive self-worth may be a process and take some time but is critical to healthy development.

UNDERSTANDING AUTISM

Do You Think Being Autistic Is Good, Bad, or You're Not Sure?

Circle one and explain why you feel that way.

GOOD

BAD

NOT SURE

UNDERSTANDING AUTISM

Using and Processing the Worksheet

Does Being Autistic Make You Different From Other Children?

Autistic children and teens may struggle with feeling they are different from others, which can affect their self-worth and create feelings of isolation. This worksheet page helps children accurately define ways they may be different from their peers and ways they are the same as their peers. Professionals and parents should allow the child to identify anything they can think of and then help the child complete this worksheet and correct any errors the child may believe, especially about feeling different from peers and viewing differences as bad.

Professionals and parents may also need to point out several ways the child is the same or like any other child. It is important to hear what the child thinks and acknowledge their feelings. It is also important to make sure the child is perceiving their situation accurately. As this worksheet is being completed, it may be beneficial to ask the child how they feel about being different from peers. Are they okay with the differences or is it something they want to change?

Being different is not bad, but believing that being different is something less than, or bad, is not healthy. It is important that autistic children view themselves positively and feel good about their qualities and traits—maybe different but never less.

UNDERSTANDING AUTISM

Does Being Autistic Make You Different from Other People?

Talk about, draw, or write what you think.

Let's write down some ways you might be different.

_____
_____
_____

Let's write down some ways you are the same.

_____
_____
_____

Using and Processing the Worksheet

Are There Certain Things You Can Do (Strengths) Because You Are Autistic?

Unfortunately, being autistic can come with others producing a long list of what is "wrong" or "bad." There is nothing wrong with being autistic, and there are noted strengths that typically accompany being autistic.

In this worksheet, it is important to give the child a chance to understand their strengths and the strengths of autistic individuals in general. It also is important to dispel thoughts and messages that have communicated being autistic as a list of deficits.

The worksheet is presented as an autistic strengths quilt with nine spaces. The child is instructed to write or draw in each space things they think can be a strength about being autistic. The child does not have to produce nine things. (They can do as many as they can think of.) The professional or parent can add strengths to the quilt.

Potential strengths include the following:

- long-term memory skills,
- direct communication,
- math,
- computer,
- musical,
- artistic skills,
- thinking in a visual way,
- hyperlexia,
- punctuality,
- honesty,
- detail oriented,
- average to above-average intelligence,
- independent thinking,
- loyalty,
- non-judgmental listening,
- extensive knowledge in specific topics,
- understanding rules and sequences,
- logical thinking, and
- intensive focus when working on a preferred activity.

Are There Certain Things You Can Do (Strengths) Because You Are Autistic?

The Autistic Strengths Quilt

Using and Processing the Worksheet

What Is It Like Playing With Other Kids When You Are Autistic?

Play skills, peer interactions, and friendship skills can be challenging areas for autistic children and teens to navigate. The following worksheets are separated into two worksheets for children and two worksheets for teens. The worksheet pages serve as assessment tools to discover more about a child's play, interactions with peers, and friendships.

The first worksheet asks the child to complete eight questions related to friendship and playing with other children. The child can write the answers, or simply give a verbal response that the professional or parent can write down. Some of the questions may be challenging for the child to answer as they may not know how to describe a friend or be able to remember their friend's names. Also, children may not accurately understand relationship levels, such as a "friend" verses an "acquaintance." The child may think someone who said hello once to them weeks ago is a good friend. These are common issues that would need to be further discussed with the child to help them have a proper understating of friendship. The second worksheet for children is the let's practice play worksheet which provides the opportunity to practice pretend play.

The second two worksheets focus on teens. The first teen worksheet asks the teen to complete eight questions about friendship. The teen can write their answers or give a verbal response. Professionals and parents will need to remember that some teens may have a difficult time answering some of the questions and the professional or parent may need to help them. The second teen worksheet provides opportunity to practice being in a conversation. A conversation guide is provided and the professional or parent can practice having a reciprocal conversation with the teen. The conversation practice can be repeated, and the teen should be encouraged to share conversation processes that feel the most comfortable for them.

UNDERSTANDING AUTISM

What Is It Like Playing With Other Kids When You Are Autistic?

(FOR CHILDREN)
Let's complete these questions

1. How would you describe a friend?

2. What does playing with other kids look like?

3. How many friends do you have?

4. What are your friends' names?

5. Do you play with adults, younger kids than you, or kids about your same age?

6. When do you play with other kids?

7. How often do you play with other kids?

8. Do you think it is easy or hard to make friends?

Let's Practice Some Play.

This is one type of play, what other ways do you like to play?

Let's pretend you are a superhero.

What is your superhero name? _____

What is your superpower? _____

What is your weakness? _____

Who is your enemy? _____

What is your costume? _____

What are your special weapons/tools? _____

Where is your hideout? _____

Let's pretend play. You be the superhero and I will be the enemy. Let's pretend to battle each other.

UNDERSTANDING AUTISM

What Is It Like Having Friends When You Are Autistic?

(FOR TEENS)
Let's complete this friend questionnaire.

1. What is a friend?

2. Do you have a boyfriend or girlfriend?

3. How many friends do you have?

4. What are your friends' names?

5. Are your friends adults, younger kids, or about your same age?

6. What do you do with your friends?

7. How often do you see your friends?

8. Do you think it is easy or hard to make friends?

Let's Practice Having a Conversation with Another Teen.

Conversation guide for practice.

Beginning:

    Say "Hello, my name is ____. What's your name?" or

    Give a compliment: "I like your shoes." or

    Say "Hi" and ask a question: "What game are you playing?"

Middle:

    Practice listening to the other persons response and replying to their response.

Ending:

    Practice ending the conversation. "I have to go. See you later."

Conversations can be tough. What are some ways that feel comfortable to you when talking to another person?

Using and Processing the Worksheet

What Do You Like to Do for Fun?

Autistic children and teens like to play, socialize with others, and have fun. They may have specific ways they prefer to play, things they like, and they may display unconventional methods of socializing and playing, but they will play. The first worksheet page provides a list of items the child or teen is asked to circle indicating the activities they like to do for fun. The professional or parent can certainly add items to this list, and the child can also add something that is not on the list. It is helpful for the child to identify things they like. Children and teens will be more successful in play and social situations if they are able to engage in doing something they like.

The second worksheet asks the child or teen to identify what they like to do for fun without others and what they would like to do with other people (friends). These are important questions for the child to answer to begin to empower them toward what they are wanting from social experiences. When trying to improve a child's social experiences, it is important to highlight the child's strengths and to listen to the child regarding what they enjoy doing and would be most interested in doing with others.

This worksheet helps professionals and parents understand what the child is thinking in terms of what they like to do and would like to do with others. Once professionals and parents have a better understanding of the child's preferences, fun experiences can be arranged for the child to participate with their peers. This worksheet also helps the child have a better awareness that they can sometimes do fun things alone and sometimes involve others in doing something fun. Most children and teens will understand they like to do things alone, but they may need help identifying what they would like to do with other people.

UNDERSTANDING AUTISM

What Do You Like to Do for Fun?

Circle all the things listed below that you like to do for fun and add anything not listed.

Play Legos   Play Video Games   Draw   Listen to Music

Play Sports   Read   Play with Pets   Play Board Games   iPad

Watch TV   Computer   Play with Dolls   Play with Toys

Go to a Movie   Complete an Art Project   Dance

Go for a Walk   Eat   Write   Talk on the Phone   Go to a Store

Anything Else?

_____

_____

_____

_____

_____

UNDERSTANDING AUTISM

What Do You Like to Do by Yourself and What Could You Do With Others?

Write down or draw fun activities you like to do by yourself.

Write down or draw fun activities you could do with a friend.

Using and Processing the Worksheet

What Animal Do You Think You Are Most Like and Why?

This worksheet is designed to provide some fun for the child or teen and possibly get to know the child better. They are instructed to think about what animal they are most like and then draw their animal inside the star shape. They are further asked to talk about why they are like the animal they chose.

It is possible that children will choose an animal they identify with in some manner. This can help the professional or parent better understand how the child feels about themselves. The professional or parent may want to complete the activity as well and share with the child what animal they identify with.

Remember to explain that drawing skills are not necessary to complete this activity or any activity in this guidebook.

UNDERSTANDING AUTISM

What Animal Do You Think You Are Most Like and Why?

Draw your animal in the star below.

UNDERSTANDING AUTISM

Using and Processing the Worksheet

If You Could Jump into Any Video Game, What One Would It Be and Why?

This worksheet is similar to the previous worksheet (draw an animal). Some children may be more interested in video games than animals. This worksheet is designed to provide some fun for the child or teen and possibly get to know the child better. They are instructed to think about a video game they would like to be a part of and then draw themselves in the video game. They are further asked to talk about what video game they chose and why they chose it.

It is possible that children will choose a video game they identify with in some manner. This can help the professional or parent better understand how the child feels about themselves. The professional or parent may want to complete the activity as well and share with the child what video game they would like to join.

Remember to explain that drawing skills are not necessary to complete this activity or any activity in this guidebook.

UNDERSTANDING AUTISM

If You Could Jump Into Any Video Game, What One Would It Be and Why?

Draw a picture of yourself in the video game.

UNDERSTANDING AUTISM

Using and Processing the Worksheet

Does the Place You Are in (Home, School, Church) Make a Difference If You Are Autistic?

Autistic children and teens will fluctuate in how much dysregulation they are experiencing depending on their environment. There are environments that present more challenges to a child and environments that will feel less challenging and more regulating. It is important for children and teens to understand the places and situations that create anxiety and dysregulation. It is also important they can identify environments that feel relaxing.

Professionals and parents will want to know this information and help prepare the child when they are going into an environment that will likely be more challenging. This worksheet page asks the child to try and identify what they feel about various environments, and then create a list of the most comfortable to the most uncomfortable environments in which they participate. Many children will have some awareness of situations or places that feel uncomfortable to them and places they like to be because they feel more relaxed. For example, they may know they feel uncomfortable at school but relaxed in their bedroom at home.

The professional or parent will likely have to remind the child of the different environments in which they participate and then allow the child to categorize the environments by comfort level. The worksheet lists three categories: comfortable, sometimes uncomfortable, and really uncomfortable. The child or teen can list several places in each category. The child or the adult working with the child can create additional categories if needed. Professionals and parents will want to process through what makes the child uncomfortable in certain environments and possibly brainstorm strategies to help the child be more successful in the uncomfortable environments.

UNDERSTANDING AUTISM

Does the Place You Are in (Home, School, Church) Make a Difference If You Are Autistic?

Talk about, draw, or write what you think.

Let's make a ranking from your most comfortable place to your most uncomfortable place to be.

Comfortable _____

Sometimes Uncomfortable _____

Really Uncomfortable _____

UNDERSTANDING AUTISM

Using and Processing the Worksheet

Who Helps Autistic Children?

On this worksheet page, children and teens are first asked to write or talk about who they believe helps autistic children. If the child is communicating this verbally, then the professional or parent should write down what the child says. It is important to note who the child perceives as helpers and keep this list as support people in the child's life. If the child or teen cannot think of anyone, the professional or parent may provide some examples of people who typically help children.

The second part of the worksheet page presents a list of some people who most commonly work with and help autistic children. The child is asked to place a check mark next to any of the people listed that have helped them. As the child indicates people, the professional or parent can talk about the specific person who has helped the child, and what type of help that person provided. This is a good worksheet to introduce children and teens to people they may be working with or will work with who can provide services and support. It is important that children feel positive about the individuals they may be working with to help them with their needs.

This worksheet also allows the child to recognize family members and friends as people who help or have helped the child. It also gives the professional working with the child the opportunity to communicate to the child how the professional can be a support for the child. Children and teens can understand and accept that there are people in their lives who will regularly be providing guidance and support.

UNDERSTANDING AUTISM

Who Helps Autistic Children?

Talk about, draw, or write what you think.

Below are examples of people who might help autistic children. Put a check beside the types of people who have helped you.

___Parents ___Teachers

___Counselors ___Family Members

___Speech Therapists ___Occupational Therapists

___Music Therapists ___Social Workers

___Play Therapists ___Coaches

___Friends ___Other People

Using and Processing the Worksheet

Does Being Autistic Mean There Are Things You Can't Do or Things You Might Do Better Than Other People?

Sometimes autistic children receive negative messages about being autistic, or about the way they may think, feel, or behave. It is important to counter the negative messages by actively helping the child feel positive about themselves and identifying the strengths they possess. The first worksheet page asks the child or teen to share what they think about being autistic in the sense of being able to do things better, or not as well as other people. The child or teen is then asked to write down all the things they think they are good at. If the child cannot think of anything, the professional or parent can assist the child in identifying things they are good at doing.

The professional or parent should take note of what the child expresses. Some of the child's thoughts may need to be addressed further and more specifically in a therapeutic setting to insure healthy self-worth. Some children and teens may struggle with low self-esteem due to their recognized differences from their neurotypical peers and/or lack of success in peer social situations.

The second worksheet page asks the child or teen to share their thoughts about autism and jobs. The child is asked to say or write down if they think being autistic will prevent them from doing certain jobs. The child or teen is then asked to draw themselves inside a circle doing the career they think they would be able to do best. The professional or parent working with the child can also offer suggestions. After the worksheets have been completed, the professional or parent should process through the child's responses and talk about the child's strengths and potential to develop more strengths. The child or teen should recognize the things they do well and feel empowered to develop additional talents.

UNDERSTANDING AUTISM

Does Being Autistic Mean There Are Things You Can't Do or Things You Might Do Better Than Other People?

Talk about, draw, or write what you think.

Write down all the things you think you are good at.

Does Being Autistic Mean There Are Jobs You Will Not Be Able to Do?

What are your thoughts?

_____

_____

Draw yourself in the circle below doing the career that you think you would be the best at.

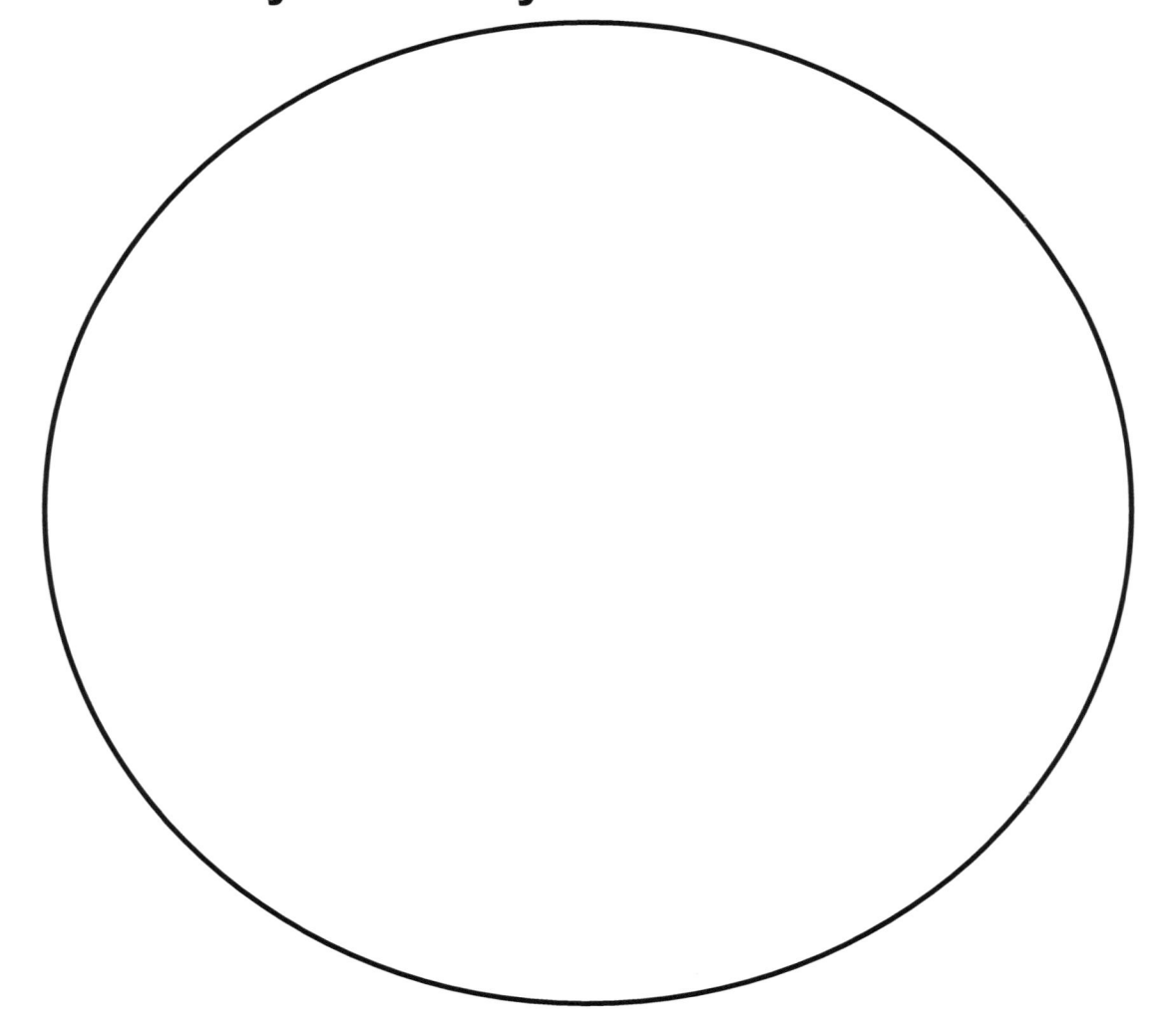

UNDERSTANDING AUTISM

Using and Processing the Worksheet

Do You Know Any Famous Autistic People? If So, List Them Below.

This is a useful worksheet page for any child or teen learning about autism. Many autistic children feel isolated. Many children also feel their disability limits them or will prevent them from being successful in life. This worksheet page asks the child to think about and list any famous person the child can think of that is autistic. It is likely the child will not be able to think of anyone. The professional or parent can list anyone they know. This can be someone in the child's local community. (It does not have to be a celebrity).

Once the child and the adult have finished listing people, the professional or parent should assist the child in accessing the link indicated on the worksheet page for a list of famous people who are autistic. The professional or parent should talk with the child about each person and their accomplishments and add some of the famous people to the child's list. The worksheet activity helps children begin to understand they do not have to feel limited because they are autistic. It also helps children discover famous and successful autistics who may serve as role models. Learning about accomplished individuals can be empowering to the child or teen. The link that is shared on the worksheet page lists successful autistic individuals from a variety of settings. Professionals and parents can also search online for additional examples.

UNDERSTANDING AUTISM

Do You Know Any Famous Autistic People? If So, List Them Below.

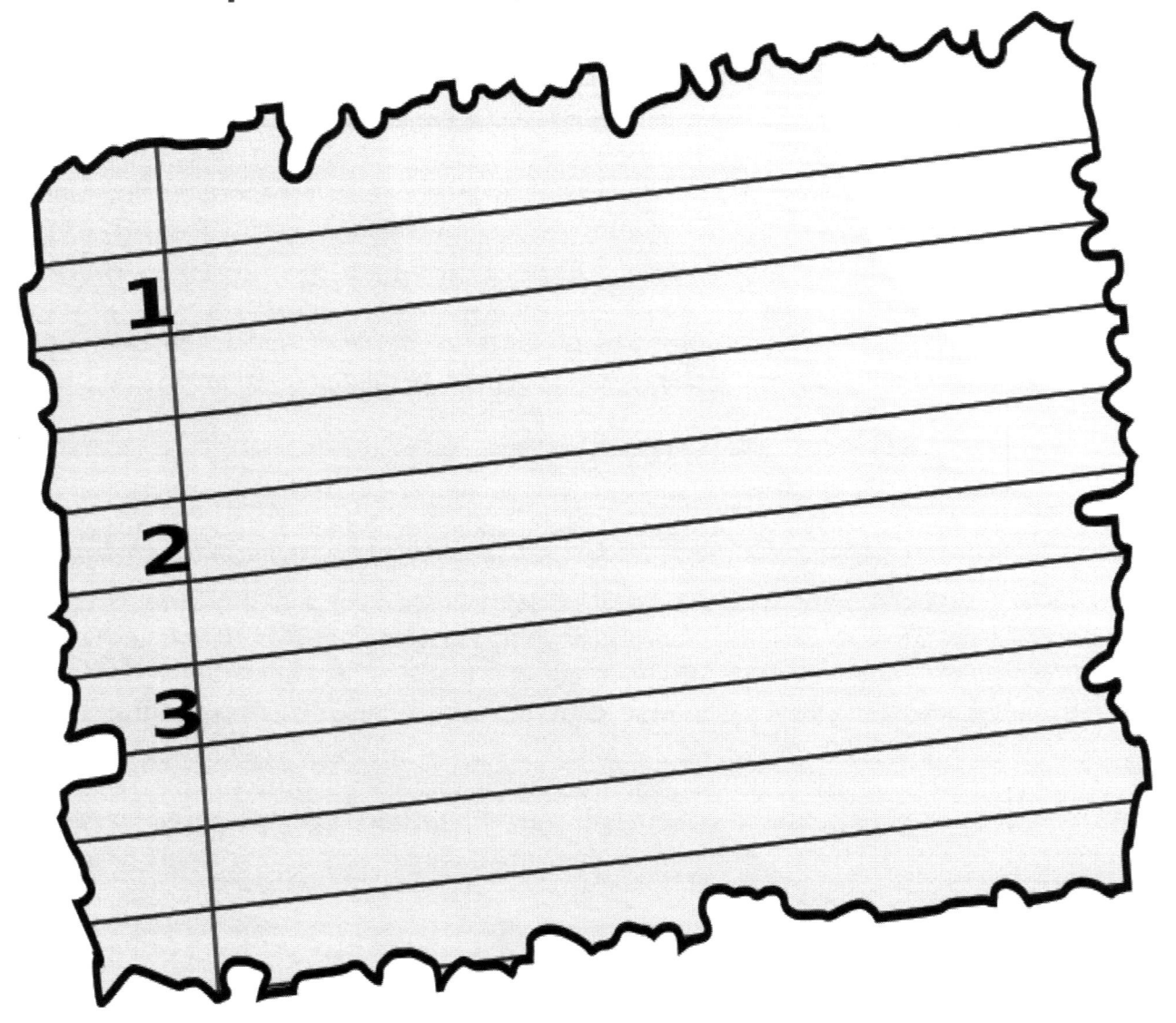

1.

2.

3.

**There are several famous autistic people.
Visit this link to see a list.**
https://blog.ongig.com/diversity-and-inclusion/famous-people-with-autism/

UNDERSTANDING AUTISM

Using and Processing the Worksheet

What Do You Want Others to Know About You?

Autistic children and teens are notoriously misunderstood and mislabeled. Often, they are not even considered in terms of their own thoughts and feelings. This worksheet gives the child or teen opportunity to share anything and everything they want others to know about them. This is an important space for the adult to listen to the child and provide value to what the child is communicating.

The child can write thoughts down, draw their thoughts, or verbally tell the professional or parent. Once the worksheet has been completed, the adult and child can discuss ways to help others better understand the child. This might involve strategies or tools that the adult and child create.

UNDERSTANDING AUTISM

What Do You Want Others to Know About You?

Write or draw your thoughts below.

UNDERSTANDING AUTISM

Using and Processing the Worksheet

What Do You Wish Others Understood About Autism?

If the child or teen has been progressing through this workbook, at this point, they have learned quite a bit about autism. This worksheet gives the child an opportunity to express what they wish others knew about autism. The child does not have to address their own autism specifically—they can express about autism in general.

Children and teens can receive a great deal of information about autism often without their parents or a professional knowing. The Internet is cluttered with information and certainly it is easy to access for many children. Autism is also discussed, presented, and highlighted in television and movies. Unfortunately, this abundance of access to information does not mean the information is always accurate or affirming.

This worksheet could be used early with a child to assess what the child currently knows and thinks about autism and where they have received their information. If any misconceptions, internalized ableism, or simply wrong information exists, the professional or parent will want to address the issue.

UNDERSTANDING AUTISM

What Do You Wish Others Understood About Autism?

Write or draw your thoughts below.

UNDERSTANDING AUTISM

Using and Processing the Worksheet

Let's Write a Letter Describing You to Someone.

    This worksheet page asks the child or teen to write a letter describing themselves to someone. If the child cannot write, they can say what they want, and the adult can write it down. The child can decide to write the letter to a real person or a generic person. The letter begins with *I am me and I'm autistic and that means*. This worksheet activity provides the opportunity for the child or teen to bring the information they have learned together and describe themselves. The child or teen should write whatever they want in the letter. The professional or parent should encourage the child to say or write down any thoughts or emotions that come to mind and think about the different things they have learned throughout this workbook.

    Once the child is finished with the letter, the child or the adult should read the letter. Ideally, the child will have a healthy conceptualization of their autistic self. The letter activity gives the professional or parent a clear view of what the child is thinking. The professional or parent should process through the letter with the child and address any misconceptions the child may still have. If the letter was addressed to a real person, the child can decide if they want to give the letter to that person. It is the child's decision as to what happens with the letter.

UNDERSTANDING AUTISM

Let's Write a Letter Describing You to Someone.

Dear _____

I am me and I am autistic and that means…

_____
_____
_____
_____
_____
_____
_____
_____
_____
_____
_____
_____
_____
_____
_____
_____
_____

UNDERSTANDING AUTISM

Using and Processing the Worksheet

What Are Some Things You Want to Remember That Make You Feel Good?

This worksheet is a good ending worksheet for the child or teen to complete as they have progressed through this workbook. The child is asked to write or draw some things they want to remember that make them feel good about themselves. It is important that autistic children carry positive messages about themselves. The child can produce anything they want— a thought, a saying, a picture— anything that helps them remember to feel good about themselves.

If the child has a difficult time producing things that make them feel good, the professional or parent can help them. Also, the professional or parent can complete the worksheet about the child and share their observations with the child.

UNDERSTANDING AUTISM

What Are Some Things You Want to Remember That Make You Feel Good?

Write or draw your thoughts below.

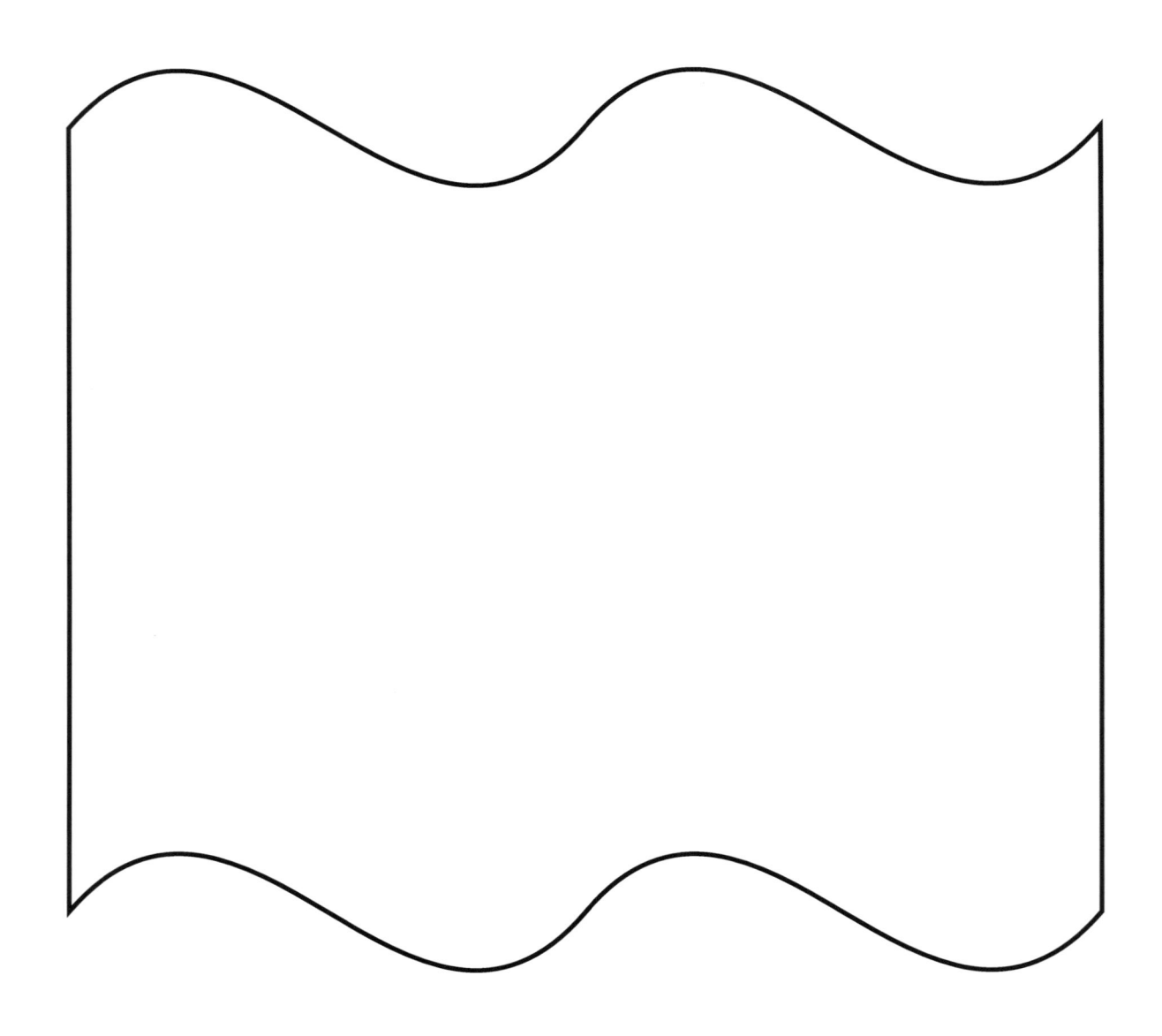

UNDERSTANDING AUTISM

Using and Processing the Worksheet

Being Autistic Can Be Awesome!

This worksheet page asks the child or teen to write or draw all the awesome things they think about themselves. Professionals and parents should also add awesome things about the child. This guidebook ends by celebrating the child and all the awesome strengths they possess!

Being Autistic Can Be *AWESOME*!

Write down some of the things that make you awesome and draw a picture of your *AWESOME* self!

Appendix: Resources

Learning About Autism Social Story

This social story can be read to kids before starting the guidebook. The social story should be read by the professional and/or parents a few times before starting the guidebook.

Some people are autistic.

I am an autistic person.

It is important for kids to learn about autism.

I can learn about autism.

When I learn about autism, it will help me understand myself better.

When I learn about autism, I will understand my feelings and my actions better.

A professional and my parents may help me understand autism.

I may use a guidebook to help me understand being autistic.

I can talk about autism.

I can ask questions about autism.

I may be different from other autistic kids.

I can learn about being autistic and that is okay.

I can learn about being autistic and that will help me.

The professional and my parents will help when I learn about autism.

I can feel good learning about autism.

UNDERSTANDING AUTISM

My Autistic Snapshot

My Name: _____

What I Think About Being Autistic: _____

My Strengths:
    1. _____
    2. _____
    3. _____

Things I Might Want to Improve:
    1. _____
    2. _____
    3. _____

Places That Are Hard for Me: _____

_____

Things That Help Me Feel Better: _____

_____

UNDERSTANDING AUTISM

How Being Autistic Affects Me: _____
_____
_____
_____

People Who Help Me With My Needs: _____
_____

Some Things That Help Me Feel Calm:
    1. _____
    2. _____
    3. _____

Some Things I Like to Do for Fun:
    1. _____
    2. _____
    3. _____

Awesome Things About Me: _____
_____
_____
_____
_____

UNDERSTANDING AUTISM

AutPlay® Autism Checklist–Revised

Child's Name
_____Age____Gender_____Date_____

  The AutPlay® Autism Checklist-Revised is a strengths-based autism screening instrument to help assess the possibility of autism and need for further evaluation. Place a check by each statement that describes your child. If you are unsure, leave the statement blank.

_____

____Seems to have their own way of communicating and interacting

____Shows or seems to have strong reactions to sensory experiences

____Seems to do things in a way that might not be expected

____Seems to view peer relationships and interactions with peers differently than might be expected

____Prefers constructive play (Legos, blocks, train track)

____Does not seem interested in and does not display pretend play

____Spends time playing alone or seems to prefer to play alone

____Prefers solitary activities

____Prefers or displays nonverbal communication

____Displays stimming (hand or finger flapping, twisting, or spinning)

____Displays stimming while talking, or looking away while talking

____Seems bored when talking with others

____Seems drawn to or prefers technology play (electronics)

____Seems to prefer sensory-based play

____Has an intense focus on specific things or subjects

____Preoccupation with one or more interests

____Prefers a routine, schedule, or planned activity

____Displays a special interest and seems not interested in things outside of the special interest

____Not as interested in social processes that may be common with peers

About the AutPlay® Autism Checklist-R

The Checklist is based in part upon the DMS-V diagnostic criteria for Autism Spectrum Disorder and focuses on viewing the child from a more strengths-based description. It is valid for children ages 4-11. The checklist is designed to be completed by a parent or other caregiver who is familiar or involved enough with the child to provide accurate feedback. Practitioners should use the checklist in the following ways:
1. as part of an autism screening procedure to determine if further evaluation is needed
2. as an assessment tool to gain further information about a child's strengths and needs
3. as an aid in developing therapy goals.

Instructions for completing the AutPlay® Autism Checklist-R

Practitioners should give the checklist to parents and/or caregivers who are familiar with the child (this might include foster parents, teachers, nannies, or other relatives). Parents and/or caregivers are instructed to complete the checklist by placing a check next to any statement they feel describes the child.

Parents and/or caregivers are not given a copy of the About the AutPlay® Autism Checklist-R (page 2). Practitioners should review and share results with parents and/or caregivers and provide recommendations.

Scoring

The AutPlay® Autism Checklist-R is not a diagnostic tool. When completing the AutPlay® Autism Checklist-R as part of an autism screening, practitioners should compare results on the checklist with other screening inventories or procedures as part of a comprehensive screening protocol and consider additional factors to determine if further evaluation is warranted.

The Checklist should not be the sole instrument used for an autism screening. The following scoring guide is designed to help inform further recommendations:

0–1	Not indicative of further evaluation
2–5	Possible referral for further evaluation
6 or above	Indicative of further evaluation

Practitioners looking for more resources for conducting autism screenings should consider conducting a child observation, a parent/child observation, and implementing additional inventories. Practitioners should refer parents and/or caregivers for a full evaluation if there is an indication of autism.

Child's Name _____ Score _____ Date _____

Identity Language Article

Play Therapists and the Terminology of Autism by Robert Jason Grant

When discussing autism, terminology is significant, and much has been discussed about the use of identity-first vs person-first language when referencing autism. An example of identity-first language is *autistic child* or *autistic individuals*. An example of person-first language is *child with autism* or *individuals with autism*.

A basic inquiry in research, writings, and comments on social media will find play therapists and other child therapists very mixed in using both types of language, but is there a right way and a wrong way? A research study by Kenny (2015) sampled 3,470 participants in the UK—a mix of autistic adults, parents of autistic children, and professionals who worked with autistic individuals. The study focused on preferred ways of describing autism and the rationale for such preferences. The term *autistic* (identity-first language) was endorsed by a large percentage of autistic adults and family members/friends and parents, but by considerably fewer professionals. *Person with autism* (person-first language) was endorsed by almost half of professionals but by fewer autistic adults and parents. None of the groups were unanimous in a preference or endorsement.

Bottema-Beutel (2020) stated that research on Australian samples has shown that autistic people rated the terms *autistic, person on the spectrum*, and *autistic person* significantly preferable than *person with autism*. Other U.S.- and U.K.-based research has shown that self-identification as autistic and awareness of the neurodiversity movement are associated with stronger preferences for the term *autistic person* over *person with autism*. In summary, research indicates the majority of autistic adults and those who support neurodiversity initiatives endorse identity-first language, parents have a greater range in endorsement of either identity-first or person-first language, and the majority of professionals tend to endorse person-first language.

I can remember when the person-first language movement was in full application. It was considered the progressive and enlightened way to refer to someone. There was quite a mindful shift to using person-first language as a way to show respect and value. This was a significant movement in medical and mental health care, which might explain some of the reason many professionals are still using person-first language. It is also true that some individuals/groups outside of autism still prefer the use of person-first language when addressing a disability or disorder. Thus, play therapists are taxed with the responsibility of understanding the particular person/issue/group they are working with and being able to switch back and forth depending on the endorsement/preference.

Further awareness for many play therapists involves the fact that most of us work with children, many children will not have processed or understood these concepts, and it will likely be the endorsement/preference of the parent the play therapist is addressing. Research has not been as clear on parents' endorsement, as parents seem more evenly divided on language endorsement/preference. To further complicate issues, an older child or teen may be in a position where they are expressing a preference and their parents prefer something else. For the play therapist, this becomes an issue in therapy that will require sensitivity to navigate.

Due to the person-first movement, I primarily used person-first language for many years, as this was identified as the respectful and professional guideline. I began to shift my language usage as I heard more from autistic adults about their preference for identity-first language. At that point, I spent a considerable amount of time integrating both preferences in my writings and trainings, trying to provide affirmation to different beliefs. More recently, I have committed to a more complete shift to using identity-first language in reference to autism. There are a couple of reasons for this:

1. Research overwhelming supports that the majority of autistic adults endorse and prefer identity-first language, and for me, this is vitally important—if the majority of individuals are expressing this is their want and preference, we should be validating (hearing and recognizing their voice).
2. As someone who is non-autistic but neurodivergent, I can identify with the awareness that there are things about me that are who I am and are not going to change with therapies, treatments, etc. I greatly appreciate when professionals understand this, and we work on what really needs to be addressed based on this understanding.

As play therapists, moving forward in our own growth, I have discovered three tips that might be helpful:

1. In the therapeutic setting, the client's voice should be heard and respected. If the client prefers certain language be used, we should honor that preference.
2. A general default should be identity-first language, and certainly this can accompany an explanation if someone inquires why you are using identify-first language. Often when I present or write, I will provide a disclaimer at the beginning that states "I am choosing to use identity-first language due to research showing that the majority of autistic adults prefer identity-first language. I realize there may be different thoughts in the audience. I respect differing views, but for our purposes today (or in this writing), I am defaulting to identity-first language for the reason I just identified."

3. Stay committed to learning and growth and pursue listening to and reading works by autistic adults who are writing, speaking, and training on the subject of autism.

In my history of work with autistic children and their families, there is one thing that has remained constant—this vulnerable population is greatly underserved in obtaining mental health services. Each time I meet a play therapist who provides therapy to autistic children, I am delighted. Whether it is addressing terminology, or any issue related to autism, we need to keep encouraging each other and growing together to help improve mental health access and services to autistic children and their families.

Bottema-Beutel, K., Kapp, S. K., Lester, J. N., Sasson, N. J., & Hand, B. N. (2020). Avoiding ableist language: Suggestions for autism researchers. *Autism in Adulthood*. doi: 10.1089/aut.2020.0014

Kenny L, Hattersley C, Molins B, Buckley C, Povey C, & Pellicano E. (2015). Which terms should be used to describe autism? Perspectives from the UK autism community. *Autism*, 20(4), 442-462. doi:10.1177/1362361315588200

Feeling List

Accepted	Afraid	Affectionate	Loyal
Angry	Miserable	Anxious	Misunderstood
Peaceful	Beautiful	Playful	Ashamed
Brave	Awkward	Calm	Proud
Capable	Quiet	Bored	Overwhelmed
Caring	Relaxed	Confused	Cheerful
Relieved	Defeated	Comfortable	Safe
Competent	Satisfied	Concerned	Mad
Depressed	Pressured	Confident	Provoked
Content	Desperate	Regretful	Courageous
Silly	Lonely	Rejected	Curious
Special	Disappointed	Remorseful	Strong
Discouraged	Disgusted	Sad	Sympathetic
Excited	Embarrassed	Shy	Forgiving
Thankful	Sorry	Friendly	Thrilled
Fearful	Stubborn	Nervous	Stupid
Glad	Understood	Frustrated	Good
Unique	Furious	Tired	Grateful
Valuable	Guilty	Touchy	Great
Hateful	Happy	Helpless	Hopeful
Wonderful	Hopeless	Humorous	Worthwhile
Unattractive	Joyful	Uncertain	Lovable
Humiliated	Uncomfortable	Loved	Hurt
Ignored	Impatient	Indecisive	Inferior
Insecure	Irritated	Jealous	Worried

AWESOME Autism Books for Children

All Cats Are on the Autism Spectrum by Kathy Hoopmann
Several cats take a playful look at the world of autism, and these fun feline friends will strike a chord with all those who are familiar with typical autistic traits, bringing to life common characteristics such as sensory sensitivities, social issues, and communication difficulties. Touching, humorous, and insightful, this book evokes all the joys and challenges of being on the autism spectrum, leaving the reader with a sense of the dignity, individuality, and potential of autistic people.

Albert Is My Friend by Dr. Linda Barboa & Jan Luck
This book is about the friendship between a young boy, Albert, who is autistic and his friend, Mary Louise. Together they describe and explain some common autism expressions at a child's level of understanding. This book presents a positive attitude and is a must read for family members, teachers, and community members. *Albert Is My Friend* is one of several books in the Albert series. Other titles include *Albert Goes to School, Albert Goes to Church,* and *Albert Builds a Friendship*.

All My Stripes by Shaina Rudolph & Danielle Royer
This is the story of Zane, an autistic zebra, who worries that his differences make him stand out from his peers. With careful guidance from his mother, Zane learns that autism is only one of many qualities that make him special. The book contains a Note to Parents by Drew Coman, PhD, and Ellen Braaten, PhD, as well as a Foreword by Alison Singer, President of the Autism Science Foundation.

A Friend Like Simon by Kate Gaynot
When an autistic child joins a mainstream school, many children can find it difficult to understand and cope with a student that is somewhat "different" from them. This story encourages other children to be mindful and patient of the differences that exist and to appreciate the positive contribution that an autistic child can make to the group.

Benji, The Bad Day, and Me by Sally J. Pla
Nothing seems to be going right for Sammy today. At school, he gets in trouble for kicking a fence, and then the cafeteria runs out of pizza for lunch. After he walks home in the pouring rain, he finds his autistic little brother Benji is having a bad day too. On days like this, Benji has a special play-box where he goes to feel cozy and safe. Sammy doesn't have a special place, and he's convinced no one cares how he feels or even notices him. But somebody is noticing and may just have an idea on how to help Sammy feel better.

AWESOME Autism Books for Teens

The Alien Logs of Super Jewels by B. K. Bradshaw
This book introduces readers to Jewels, a young teen with Asperger's Syndrome. Teens on the spectrum will undeniably relate to her strengths, challenges, and her view of the world, and hopefully discover their own superhero selves. The strength of this book is in its lighthearted, yet vividly honest, believable, and informative style. In this sense, it is a useful resource for parents, teachers, and other adults working with teens on the spectrum.

Anything but Typical by Nora Raleigh Baskin
This story is told entirely from the point of view of Jason, an autistic boy who is a creative-writing whiz and deft explainer of literary devices, but markedly at a loss in social interactions with neurotypicals both at school and at home. He is most comfortable in an online writing forum called Storyboard, where his stories kindle an e-mail-based friendship with a girl. The author describes Jason's attempts to interpret body language and social expectations, and ultimately how Jason moves through his failures and triumphs with the same depth of courage and confusion of any boy his age.

The Someday Birds by Sally J. Pla
Charlie's perfectly ordinary life has been unraveling ever since his war journalist father was injured in Afghanistan. When his father heads from California to Virginia for medical treatment, Charlie reluctantly travels cross-country with his boy-crazy sister, unruly brothers, and a mysterious new family friend. He decides that if he can spot all the birds that he and his father were hoping to see someday along the way, then everything might just turn out okay. The tale is equal parts madcap road trip, coming-of-age story for an autistic boy who feels he doesn't understand the world, and an uplifting portrait of a family overcoming a crisis.

How to Be Human: Diary of an Autistic Girl by Florida Frenz
With powerful words and pictures, Florida Frenz chronicles her journey figuring out how to read facial expressions, how to make friends, and how to juggle all the social cues that make school feel like a complicated maze. Diagnosed with autism as a two-year-old, Florida is now an articulate 15-year-old whose explorations into how kids make friends, what popularity means, and how to handle peer pressure will resonate with any preteen. For those wondering what it's like inside an autistic child's head, Florida's book provides amazing insight and understanding. Reading how she learns to be human makes us all feel a little less alien.

AWESOME Websites for Children and Teens

www.autismgames.com.au

www.whizkidgames.com

www.autismgames.org

www.neal.fun

www.onlinedollhouses.com

www.onlinesandtray.com

www.onlinepuppets.org

www.wrongplanet.net

www.aspergersteenchat.com

AWESOME YouTube Channels

AutPlay Therapy

Wrong Planet

Clair Mellenthin

Autism Self Advocacy Network

Autistic Tyla

Liana Lowenstein

Aspergers from the Inside

Yo Samdy Sam

Kati Morton

Neurodivergent Rebel

Tammi Van Hollander

Lisa Dion, Synergetic Play Therapy Institute

AWESOME Autism Apps for Children and Teens

Snappy Kids
Snap's Stories about feelings is a mobile app of therapeutic stories and activities intended to help kids learn about and manage their own feelings. Anger, worry, fear, and sadness are among the feelings addressed in the stories and activities. The app comes with two stories: "What's Your Lava Level?," about managing frustration and anger, and "Worried Wendall," about worry or anxiety. A third story, "Don't Explode, Snap!," also addresses anger and is available as an in-app purchase.

Puppet Pals 1 and 2
This app allows children to create their own unique shows with animation and audio in real time. They pick out their actors and backdrops, drag them on to the stage, and tap record. The child can move the puppets/actors around, and audio can be recorded in real time for playback later.

Fingle
In this app, players explore the intimate touch of each other's fingers with Fingle's two-player puzzles. Break the ice or engage friends to get awkwardly close. Two players drag up to five buttons of one color onto their matching targets; their movement makes it impossible to avoid contact, creating intimate moments with intertwined hands.

Drive Focus
This app focuses on driver training in a fun and engaging format. Teens will learn essential visual search skills and strategies with interactive video technology. Drive Focus teaches teens to identify items on the roadway and how to decide when they are important.

EQ Game
This app will challenge a teen's emotional literacy with its highly interactive card game format. There are quirky animations, character-filled illustrations, and quizzes. The EQ Game is designed to improve a teen's vocabulary of emotions. There is even a narrated story with a character exploring the Trichy world of emotions.

Felt Board
Design scenes, dress up characters, and let the imagination soar as children invent their own stories. Create characters by selecting skin color, hair, and facial features. Choose from a wide variety of costumes, settings, and props for hours of magical make-believe play.

AWESOME Autism Games for Children

Should You Eat Cookies in the Bathtub?
This engaging and interactive game may be played in three different ways, depending on the players' level of knowledge, expressive language, social awareness, and abstract thinking. The game consists of two decks: 26 Behavior Cards and 26 Context Cards. Many card combinations will stimulate discussion, perhaps of specific instances. Others will almost always be inappropriate regardless of context (hitting, for example) and some are appropriate activities to reinforce. A few may be just silly and fun to laugh over.

Journey to Friendsville
A fun and interactive board game where children can learn social skills and how to develop friendships. As they play the game, children move through towns that represent the skills taught in the game, such as Fairhaven and Conversation City. On the way, players earn tokens with pictures of "friends" on them. The "friends" are placed in Friendsville in the center of the board to await the arrival of the players.

Feelings Fair
This board game is specifically designed to give children important skills for recognizing feelings in themselves and others, expressing feelings in a mature way, and handling difficult situations that involve strong or negative feelings. The game board has all the attractions of a carnival or fair. Players journey through the fair, picking cards that enhance their understanding and skills for expressing feelings. Some cards ask the players to describe or act out a feeling, and the other players must guess the feeling. Other cards ask participants to solve problems involving feelings.

Feelings Playing Cards
Feelings Playing Cards displays 30 different feelings. Instructions are included for 15 different games, so teens will never grow tired of playing with these durable cards. They can be used in group or individual counseling. Each card has a face, number, and suit, so you can use these as regular playing cards, too. The cards are slightly larger than a regular deck, sized 4 1/2"x 3 1/2".

Hedbanz
Hedbanz is a fun, interactive game that promotes communication and social interaction and develops deductive reasoning skills. Teens ask yes or no questions to figure out if the cartoon on their head is an animal, food, or man-made object.

AWESOME Neurodiversity Affirming Resources

Autism Self Advocacy Network: www.autisticadvocacy.org

Foundations for Divergent Minds: www.divergentminds.org

Different Brains: www.differentbrains.org

Autistic Women and Nonbinary Network: www.awnnetwork.org

Neurodiversity Network: www.neurodiversitynetwork.net

AutPlay Therapy: www.autplaytherapy.com

The Art of Autism: www.the-art-of-autism.com

Organization for Autism Research: www.researchautism.org

Neuroclastic: www.neuroclastic.com

Neurodiversity Hub: www.neurodiversityhub.org

The Neurodiversity Podcast: www.neurodiversitypodcast.com

Communication First: www.communicationfirst.org

Lessons from the Playroom Podcast: www.synergeticplaytherapy.com/podcasts

Autism in Black Podcast: www.autisminblack.org/podcast

Actually Autistic Podcast: www.actuallyautistic.home.blog

Autism and Neurodiversity Podcast: www.jasondebbie.com

Neuroverse by Groktopus Podcast: www.neuroverse.transistor.fm

Neurotribes by Steve Silberman

Uniquely Human by Barry M. Prizant

Divergent Mind: Thriving in a World That Wasn't Designed for You by Jenara Nerenberg

Sincerely, Your Autistic Child: What People on the Autism Spectrum Wish Their Parents Knew About Growing Up, Acceptance, and Identity by Emily Paige Ballou

Loud Hands: Autistic People, Speaking by Julia Bascom

NeuroDiversity: The Birth of an Idea by Judy Singer

References

American Music Therapy Association. (2021). *About music therapy.* https://www.musictherapy.org

American Occupational Therapy Association. (2021). *About occupational therapy.* https://www.aota.org/About-Occupational-Therapy.aspx

American Psychiatric Association. (2014). *Diagnostic and statistical manual of mental disorders* (5th ed.). American Psychiatric Publishing

The Art of Autism (2021). *What is autism?* https://the-art-of-autism.com/what-is-autism/

Association for Play Therapy. (2021). *About play therapy.* https://www.a4pt.org

Attwood, T., & Garnett, M. (2013). *CBT to help young people with Asperger's syndrome (autism spectrum disorder) to understand and express affection.* Jessica Kingsley Publishers

Autism Self Advocacy Network. (2021). *About autism.* https://autisticadvocacy.org/about-asan/about-autism/

Autism Society of America. (2021). *What is autism?* https://www.autism-society.org/what-is/

Autistic Women and Nonbinary Network. (2021). *Information and resources for newly diagnosed or recognized autistic women and nonbinary individuals.* https://awnnetwork.org/wp-content /uploads/2019/05 /AWNNetworkWelcomeautisticadultspacket.pdf

Brown, H. M., Stahmer, A. C., Dwyer, P., & Rivera, S. (2021). Changing the story: How diagnosticians can support a neurodiversity perspective from the start. *Autism, 25*(5), 1171–1174. https://doi.org/10.1177/13623613211001012

Cassidy, S., Bradley, P., Robinson, J., Allison, C., McHugh, M., & Baron-Cohen, S. (2014). Suicidal ideation and suicide plans or attempts in adults with Asperger's syndrome attending a specialist diagnostic clinic: A clinical cohort study. *The Lancet Psychiatry, 1*(2), 142-147. https://doi:10.1016/s2215-0366(14)70248-2

Centers for Disease Control and Prevention. (2021). *Autism spectrum disorder (ASD).* https://www.cdc.gov/ncbddd/autism/index.html

Cruz, M. (2021). Autism, sensory experiences, and family culture. In E. P. Ballou, S. daVanport, and M. G. Onaiwu (Eds.), *Sincerely your autistic child* (pp. 157-166). Beacon Press

Goering S. (2015). Rethinking disability: the social model of disability and chronic disease. *Current reviews in musculoskeletal medicine*, 8(2), 134–138. https://doi.org/10.1007/s12178-015-9273-z

Grant, R. J., Barboa, L., Luck, J., & Obrey, E. (2021). *The complete guide to becoming autism friendly: Working with individuals, groups, and organizations.* Routledge

Grant, R. J. (2021). *AutPlay Autism Checklist Revised (AACR)*, https://autplaytherapy.com/about-autplay-therapy/resources/

Grant, R. J. (2017). *AutPlay therapy for children and adolescents on the autism spectrum: a behavioral play-based approach.* Routledge

Gratton, F. V., & Cheaney, H. (2020). *Supporting transgender autistic youth and adults: A guide for professionals and families.* Jessica Kingsley Publishers

Haruvi-Lamdan, N., Horesh, D., & Golan, O. (2018). PTSD and autism spectrum disorder: Co-morbidity, gaps in research, and potential shared mechanisms. *Psychological Trauma: Theory, Research, Practice, and Policy*, 10(3), 290–299. https://doi.org/10.1037/tra0000298

Higashida, N. (2013). *The reason I jump.* Random House

Lambert, M. (2018). *What the social model of disability can tell us about autism.* The American Association of People with Disabilities. https://www.aapd.com/what-the-social-model-of-disability-can-tell-us-about-autism/

Lowry, M. (2021). *Strengths-based autism diagnostic criteria.* Child & Adolescent Psychological Evaluations, LLC. https://www.mattlowrylpp.com

Miller, A. & Smith, T. C. (2014). *101 tips for parents of children with autism: Effective solutions for everyday challenges.* Jessica Kingsley Publishers

Milestones Autism Resource. (2021). *Self-advocacy.* https://www.milestones.org/get-started/for-individuals/self-advocacy

Moseley, K. L., Freed, G. L., Bullard, C. M., & Goold, S. D. (2007). Measuring African American parents' cultural mistrust while in a healthcare setting: A pilot study. *Journal of the National Medical Association*, 991(1), 15–21

Nelson, C. (2020). *Neurodiversity is respect*. Divergent Minds. https://www.divergentminds.org/neurodiversity-is-respect/

Notbohm, E., & Zysk, V. (2004). *1001 great ideas for teaching and raising children with autism spectrum disorders*. Future Horizons

Ohl, A. (2017). Predictors of employment status among adults with autism spectrum disorder. *American Journal of Occupational Therapy*, 71(4_Supplement_1). https://doi.org/10.5014/ajot.2017.71s1-po3090

Pattoni, L. (2012). *Strengths-based approaches for working with individuals*. https://www.iriss.org.uk/resources/insights/strengths-based-approaches-working individuals

People with Disability Australia (2021). *Social model of disability*. https://pwd.org.au/

Rapp, C., Saleebey, D., & Sullivan, P. W. (2008). The future of strengths-based social work practice. In D. Saleebey (Ed.), *The strengths perspective in social work practice* (4th ed.). Pearson Education

Siri, K., & Lyons, T. (2010). *Cutting edge therapies for autism*. Skyhorse Publishing

Stoerkel, E. (2021). *What is a strengths based approach?* https://positivepsychology.com/strengths-based-interventions/

Vormer, C. (2020). *Connecting with the autism spectrum: How to talk, how to listen, and why you shouldn't call it high functioning*. Rockridge Press

Walker (2021) *What is autism?* Neuroqueer: The writings of Dr. Nick Walker. https://neuroqueer.com/what-is-autism/

About Dr. Robert Jason Grant

Dr. Grant is a Licensed Professional Counselor, National Certified Counselor, Registered Play Therapist Supervisor, and Certified Autism Specialist. Dr. Grant specializes in working with children, adolescents, and families, including working with autistic children, neurodivergent children, and those diagnosed with ADHD and other developmental disabilities. He is the creator of AutPlay® Therapy, an integrative family play therapy approach. He is also a Certified Autism Movement Therapy and trained in EMDR (Eye Movement Desensitization and Reprocessing) Therapy, a Post Traumatic Stress Disorder/trauma-related therapy for children and adults.

Dr. Grant is an international speaker and keynote presenter, having presented for the American Counseling Association, Association for Play Therapy, American Mental Health Counselors Association, and The World Autism Congress. He is a multi-published author of several articles, book chapters, and books including the following titles:

AutPlay® Therapy for Children and Adolescents on the Autism Spectrum

Play-Based Interventions for Autism Spectrum Disorder

Understanding Sensory Processing Challenges, A Neurodiversity Affirming Workbook for Children and Teens

Understanding Autism Spectrum Disorder, A Neurodiversity Affirming Workbook for Children and Teens

Understanding ADHD: A Neurodiversity Affirming Workbook for Children and Teens

AutPlay® Therapy Play and Social Skills Groups: A Ten Session Model

Play Therapy Theories and Perspectives: Diversity of Thought in the Field

Dr. Grant is a founding board member for the non-profit organization Stars for Autism. He currently serves on the board of directors (president-elect) for the Association for Play Therapy. He is also a part-time instructor in the Play Therapy Certificate program at Mid America Nazarene University (MNU). Dr. Grant is a Certified Behavioral Life Coach through the PeopleKeys® program and provides life coaching, consultations, and play therapy supervision services. He is also a Board Certified Telepractice Specialist providing therapy and coaching through tele processes.

www.robertjasongrant.com

Additional Products by Dr. Robert Jason Grant

BOOKS
- *AutPlay® Therapy for Children and Adolescents on the Autism Spectrum: A Behavioral Play-Based Approach*
- *Play-Based Interventions for Autism Spectrum Disorder and Other Developmental Disabilities*
- *AutPlay Therapy Play and Social Skill Groups: A Ten Session Model*
- *Understanding Sensory Processing: A Neurodiversity Affirming Workbook for Children and Teens*
- *Understanding ADHD: A Neurodiversity Affirming Workbook for Children and Teens*
- *Let's Play: A Social Connection Book Game*
- *Play Therapy Theories and Perspectives: Diversity of Thought in the Field*
- *The Complete Guide to Becoming an Autism Friendly Professional: Working*
- *Implementing Play Therapy with Groups*

TRAININGS
- The AutPlay Therapy Certification Program
- Autism and Trauma: AutPlay® Therapy and Beyond
- Using Sandtrays with Autistic Children and Adolescents
- A Look at a Book: Integrating Play Therapy and Bibliotherapy
- Using Play Therapy to Address Sensory Processing Challenges
- Play Therapy Interventions for Autistic and other Neurodivergent Children
- Using Story Methods in Play Therapy: An Integrative Approach
- Understanding Ableism and Neurodiversity in Play Therapy
- AutPlay Play and Social Skills Groups
- Family Play Therapy: Approaches and Interventions
- Playrooms in Motion: Movement Interventions in Play Therapy
- Integrating Apps in Play Therapy: Working with Autistic and Neurodivergent Children

www.autplaytherapy.com

The Virtual Sandtray App AutPlay® Package

The Virtual Sandtray App (VSA) is a new media interpretation of a physical sandtray. It is a new and exciting way to bring sandtray therapy to places not convenient for physical sandtray therapy, such as hospitals, disaster areas, in-home therapy, and travel. The app provides new opportunities to work with clients, such as those physically unable to access a standard tray, those who are unable to work with sand due to sensory processing reasons, and those who will not work with a traditional sandtray.

The Virtual Sandtray App (VSA) was created by Dr. Jessica Stone and is one example of a technology tool that can be used with autistic children and adolescents. AutPlay® Therapy and the VSA partnered to create an expansion pack within the VSA app that is specifically designed for autistic children. The expansion pack includes several models/miniatures, which were designed or added to better represent interests and/or experiences of autistic children and adolescents. The expansion pack also includes 30 directive tray prompts designed to help with social/emotional needs, regulation, and connection.

Through the AutPlay® expansion pack, the therapist can implement one of the 30 directive tray prompts to align with therapy goals for their autistic client. These prompts are specifically designed to use with the functions of the VSA including models/miniatures and to target primary issues such as social/emotional needs, regulation challenges, and relationship/connection work.

Sample Select Models in the AutPlay Therapy Pack

Lego type building bricks	Electronics	Minecraft-type characters	Puzzles
Emoticons (with feeling words)	Emoticons (without feeling words)	Family members	Medial equipment

For more information, visit www.sandtrayplay.com.

The AutPlay® Therapy Certification Program

AutPlay® Therapy is a specialized play therapy approach for working with autistic children, neurodivergent children and adolescents, and children with developmental disabilities. AutPlay® was created by Dr. Robert Jason Grant to address the unique needs of neurodivergent children and adolescents who enter a therapeutic process with a licensed mental health practitioner.

AutPlay® is an integrative family play therapy approach with theoretical underpinnings in humanistic, family systems, developmental, and cognitive behavioral theories. Various play therapy theories (child-centered play therapy, filial therapy, theraplay, family play therapy, and cognitive behavioral play therapy) and relational methods are integrated into protocol, all of which incorporate evidence-based practices and empirical support for working with autistic and neurodivergent children.

The AutPlay® Certification Program coverage includes symptomology, special considerations, an overview of neurodevelopmental disorders, an intensive examination of the AutPlay® protocol including the phases of therapy, assessment strategies, target treatment areas, parent involvement and training, and limit setting procedures. Completing certified provider requirements further involves learning about the AutPlay® Follow Me Approach (FMA), which is designed for children with higher needs and engagement struggles. Participants engage in experiential activities, role-play practice, case conceptualization, and therapy planning as they complete their requirements to become a certified provider.

More specific content and requirements for the AutPlay® Therapy Certification Program can be viewed on the AutPlay® Therapy website (www.autplaytherapy.com). A current list of providers who have completed the AutPlay Therapy Certification Program is maintained and displayed on the AutPlay® website as well.

Notes Sheets

UNDERSTANDING AUTISM

Notes Sheet

UNDERSTANDING AUTISM

Notes Sheet

UNDERSTANDING AUTISM

Notes Sheet

Made in the USA
Monee, IL
21 January 2023

25820905R00077